D1535502

WITHDRAWN

Impressions of Lincoln and the Civil War

A FOREIGNER'S ACCOUNT

IMPRESSIONS OF
LINCOLN
AND THE
CIVIL WAR

A FOREIGNER'S ACCOUNT

By the Marquis Adolphe de Chambrun

TRANSLATED FROM THE FRENCH BY
General Aldebert de Chambrun

RANDOM HOUSE, NEW YORK

PREFACE

THE FOLLOWING news-letters, with their vivid description of Washington during the Civil War and eyewitness portraits of outstanding personalities including President Lincoln, have recently come into my hands.

This correspondence was addressed to my mother, Martha de Corcelle, a direct descendant of Lafayette through his youngest daughter. When the youthful General was waging the Virginian campaign which culminated in the victory of Yorktown, he asked that his child whose birth took place in France at that time be named Virginia. She shared her father's imprisonment at Olmutz and acted as hostess during his retirement at La Grange, his country place near Paris which now belongs to our branch of the family.

The hospitable roof of La Grange became a haven for seekers of political liberty, whether Polish, Irish or Italian.

Like all persons who came under Virginia's influence, my mother was early imbued with the traditions of freedom. These ideals crystallized and rooted themselves solidly through her friendship with Alexis de Tocqueville, author of *American Democracy in the United States*, a volume which first revealed to European readers the theory of free popular government as conceived among the British colonists overseas.

De Tocqueville introduced her future husband to my mother. He was Adolphe, Marquis de Chambrun, a native of Auvergne, that same mountainous region which gave birth to Lafayette. The cult of this apostle of freedom formed a lasting bond between the young couple who were married June 11, 1857, only a score of years after Lafayette's death.

Trained as a lawyer and journalist my father had already published political pamphlets containing harsh criticism of "Napoléon le Petit," then firmly established as Emperor of France but never recognized by such men as de Tocqueville, Thiers, Victor Hugo and my grandfather de Corcelle.

Realizing the impossibility of practicing law in his own country and though he did not know a word of English, my father came to a drastic decision. In December, 1864, he went to Liverpool and embarked for the United States in the hope of finding a congenial occupation with the possibility of preparing a home for his wife and five-year-old daughter, my sister Thérèse.

His plans were approved by the French Minister of Foreign Affairs, Edouard Drouyn de Lhuys, frequently mentioned throughout my father's correspondence as D. de L., a man of enlightened mind and long diplomatic experience. He had been Ambassador to England and, for years, held the portfolio of Minister of Foreign Affairs. He was naturally eager to obtain the report of an impartial observer on the progress of the war between North and South and also learn the real truth concerning what was happening in Mexico, where Napoleon III[1] was bent on placing Archduke

---

[1] Louis-Napoleon, son of Louis Bonaparte, King of Holland, took so active a part in French and Italian politics that it brought him a sentence of imprisonment for life in a French fortress. After making his escape, he established himself in Rome, where the prestige of his name aided the supporters of Italian unity to free the peninsula from Austrian rule and domination of the Papal States. This attitude earned him great popularity, so that, after the fall of Louis Philippe's regime, he was chosen as President of the French Republic. On December 2, 1852, an audacious *coup d'état* established him Emperor of the French. His Court, presided over by the beautiful Empress Eugénie, became the most brilliant in Europe.

The ambition of both sovereigns led them to embark on the intrigues of the Habsburg succession with a view to establish the Austrian Archduke Maximilian on the perilous Mexican throne. This enterprise was backed by a large French expeditionary force and ended in the tragic death of the would-be ruler under the guns of a firing squad at Queretaro (1867). Misfortune continued with the Austrian defeat of Sadowa and culminated in the Franco-Prussian war. The catastrophe of Sedan forced Napoleon III's abdication. He died in 1873 at Chiselhurst, where he was hospitably received by Queen Victoria, whose ally he had been in the Crimean War.

Maximilian of Austria on the perilous imperial throne.

Unlike most foreign military or diplomatic envoys, who were partisans of the Southern cause, my father, who had an innate horror of enforced servitude, was a staunch supporter of the Federal Government. Eventual victory was doubtful when he left France, but on landing in New York the tide had begun to turn northward.

Every Sunday he wrote his wife in Paris until she herself joined him at 1329 G Street, a small house where my brother and I saw the light, respectively, in December, 1875, and July, 1872.

During my boyhood I heard much from my parents of their association with Abraham Lincoln, Sumner, Stanton, Grant, Garfield and other notables, but even after my father's death in 1891, and until last year, I remained ignorant of the fact that he had set down all his first impressions in writing.

It was not until my sister Thérèse[2] died in Algiers only two years ago, after instituting me her Executor and Residuary legatee, that I found among a heap of old magazines, maps and newspapers, a large dilapidated book with dark mottled pasteboard covers such

---

[2] In 1895 my sister Thérèse married Count Pierre Savorgnan de Brazza, the celebrated explorer to whose patient and peaceful efforts France owes her vast settlements in Central Africa.

as was currently used for keeping household accounts during the latter half of the past century.

On opening it, my attention was at once arrested by these startling lines set down in my mother's familiar handwriting:

ADOLPHE'S LETTERS TO ME
FROM DECEMBER 20, 1864 TO JUNE 13, 1865

Laying aside other occupations, I plunged into this record of far-off days, fascinated by the penetrating character study of President Lincoln, whose rare personality my father seems to have divined at their first meeting.

Small wonder that my sister, on leaving her old home in Paris to establish herself in North Africa with her husband, Savorgnan de Brazza, should have taken away this memento of her parents' early married life, more precious to her for sentimental reasons than for their obvious historical interest.

These letters, carefully preserved in proper sequence, breathe throughout a refreshing spirit of marital affection. In this respect they strikingly resemble Lafayette's correspondence with his wife during the Virginia campaign. Both writers feel confident that nothing they say about military affairs, however technical, will leave their respective readers indifferent; what interests the husband must necessarily appeal to the wife.

A subtle difference may be noticed in the opening phrases. Lafayette begins: *"Dear heart."* My father chooses a more spiritual form of endearment: *"My dear soul."* In his case also the French use of *thou* instead of *you* lends more affectionate familiarity to the correspondence.

GENERAL DE CHAMBRUN

Impressions of Lincoln and the Civil War

A FOREIGNER'S ACCOUNT

ON BOARD THE *China*
December 31, 1864

The boat is about to weigh anchor tomorrow; so I can send this letter to Paris from the post-office of Queenstown in Ireland. I profit by the occasion with readiness, to give news of myself, register my impressions and tell you once again I love you dearly.

My health is excellent, the sea calm and there is little sickness among passengers. Personally I felt nothing but a slight spell of dizziness before dinner, not worth mentioning. If this state of things continues, I shall get through without a qualm of apprehension. The *China* is a very large ship capable of accommodating five hundred passengers. In first class, we are only forty-five or fifty, which is very few. Three or four speak French, the rest not a word. They are all American or English. The Americans are thorough-bred Yankees; they hope to find good news of Sherman in Queenstown.

Here is our daily life: breakfast before ten, lunch at midday, dinner at four, tea at seven; this means we eat all day long and I, who have a horror of this regime, ate meals like an ogre both at noon and at four. The air is brisk and probably stimulates appetite. Time is passed in three places: on deck, in the dining room where the passengers often lounge about —a gallery sixty feet long and twenty wide—or in the cabin, where there are two beds; but, if at Queenstown many passengers do not come aboard, I shall be alone until we reach New York. Not very impressive these surroundings! My only thought is of you. Rest assured that such thoughts instead of being sorrowful do me lots of good. Calling up your image gives me an emotion so strong, sweet and deep that it fills all my being. I took your dear picture from my trunk, that of our darling daughter also, kissed them and put both into my pocketbook so they will always be with me.

Dear soul, be strong, I beg you, and believe that I shall be so myself. Do not be too angry if you hear me attacked; such outbreaks are only explosions of bad temper; they will pass. You know how changeable opinion is. We have only to do well and let others talk as they please. Do not forget this maxim; it is my parting advice. I have not, I think, forgotten anything else.

Adieu, adieu, dear soul. I take you to my heart without even repeating again that I love you; you must be sure enough of that!

Sur le China Samedi 31 décembre 7 heures du soir

Mimi chérie; le bateau va relâcher
demain matin à Queenstown en
Irlande; il est possible d'écrire par la
poste de cette ville à Paris; j'en profite
avec un empressement que tu comprendras
dans priera pour te donner de mes
nouvelles et te parler de mes
impressions et te dire encore que je t'aime
bien fort.

Mes nouvelles sont excellentes; la mer
est très bonne et tu es peu malade;
pour moi je n'ai rien ressenti qu'un
petit moment d'étourdissement avec

January 13, 1865

I have at last set foot on American soil, that promised land, from now on the main object of my study. So the time has come to be energetic and try, if possible, to be intelligent. *Hic opus hic labor*—ask your brother to translate. Savannah has been taken. They say, this morning, that Charleston will soon share the same fate. Everyone rejoices at the turn of events. The latest war news seems excellent. The question on every tongue is how far has Sherman progressed? Some say that he has already reached Branchville, an important position between Augusta and Charleston. Should this prove true, he will make his entry there before long. Having been more culpable than any other Southern town during this war full of abominations, her fall will cause a burst of enthusiasm throughout the whole country. It seems certain that, from now on, the war will be waged without pause until the South is shattered, no matter what sacrifices this effort may entail. Never will the Northern armies let go their hold. It is utterly insane to believe the contrary. I cannot get over the stupidity of our French correspondents. Were I the Government, I should oblige every newspaper to send over here the reporters

5

who deal out such nonsense to the world and force each and all of them to spend a few days in New York and then go back. Two weeks of seasickness might perhaps be punishment enough for past folly.

February 13th

Everyone here is eagerly awaiting events from South Carolina, expecting news of Sherman's advance. This evening, the anxiety is over. Competent judges declare that the game is won. The capture of Charleston is but a question of days. The town is surrounded and forced to surrender, for want of supplies. This campaign will produce unexpected results as yet unforeseen. Today, I met several foreign observers who constitute themselves experts in military matters; from what they say, Sherman's campaign is a work of genius. He surely possesses the sacred fire. What seems strange: this West Point graduate, whose professional aptitudes are denied by his best friends and who is declared crazy by many others, has suddenly revealed himself as possessing an extraordinary combination of soldierly gifts. His political opinions are moderate. I will look up his photograph and send it tomorrow.

As to the aspect of New York, the port is magnificent: a veritable forest of vessels of all sorts and sizes.

6

These are obscured now and then by a great black mass—an armored cruiser or steel-embossed fortress. The entire harbor is dotted with floating batteries or small fortifications, which are built on every islet, sometimes even constructed on piles. So far, I have seen little of the town itself, but enough to be able to say that it is quite unlike any European sister town.

February 21st

My last letter told you of Sherman's march and the results that were expected from its success. I can now write that all South Carolina is entirely subdued. It is hard to conceive how the Rebels could have been so easily routed. The country around Savannah is nothing but one vast swamp. The roads are built on trestles; the Confederates did not even cut them, which would have been an easy matter. I have been given much precise information about Sherman's army. It is first class, principally made up of Westerners, a horde of men who are not only six-footers, but often measure more than that. These men are used to all kinds of work and are exceedingly good at enduring fatigue. It is they who took Vicksburg and have been in the field now for four years.

The country is in a state of ecstasy. No future tense is needed, the end is here! A series of terrible blows

7

will fall upon the South and the joy expressed is un-bounded. National pride is young, strong and naive. Yesterday, this gave rise to an amusing incident. There are some English officers here, tall gentlemen, very stiff and proud, who love their country as much as the Americans love their own. In the parlor, we were talk-ing on the eternal subject: politics. Three or four Americans—one especially—said to the English who were present: "Well, now that we are the first nation in the world, thanks to our Army and our Navy, we shall go over to England and punish you all for the harm you have been doing us during these last four years." At this, one of the English officers rose haughtily and, walking up to the American, said: "Here is my visiting card. When you come to London, I invite you to dine at my club, because I feel sure that if you ever get there, you will have to take the Cunard Line." The American orator was so stupefied that everybody burst out laughing.

WASHINGTON
February 22nd

I was happily inspired to stop first in New York and try my wings before attempting to fly. It helped me to get acquainted with the country. As for the language, it was indispensable. I would defy any

Frenchman who knows only his own tongue to make his way in the interior. Not a word of French will he ever hear; there is nothing to guide him, not a single placard nor timetable at the railway station, not an employee in uniform; the traveler must rely on himself as a pathfinder.

Here is my itinerary. You can follow me on the map. I left New York at 11.30. The Hudson once crossed, the train is boarded at Jersey City. The river is about three kilometers wide here, which is the point where I left the *China*. The railway runs straight to Philadelphia, where it stops. There a narrow-gauge track, much like the one that, starting from Place de la Concorde, connects Paris and Versailles, links this end of Philadelphia with the station at the other extremity of the town. I almost got left behind; having inquired which of the four omnibuses in waiting I should take, my kind informant, it turned out, knew as little as I did. After traveling fifteen minutes in the direction indicated, I learned that I had boarded the wrong car and panted back just in time to leap on the right one. Finally, with all the other passengers, I arrived safely in Baltimore. There, another transfer took place but it went better: four horses were hitched to each railroad car; we had only to stay quiet until, after much bumping, the train for Washington was formed.

But the worst difficulty came on our arrival, at half-past eleven. I must add that since early morning we had been accorded but five minutes in which to eat in helter-skelter fashion. I was really famished, so I directed my steps to a well-recommended hotel. The only accommodation was what they called their *sleeper*, a sort of dormitory with twenty-five or thirty beds—like a French boarding school. The "sleeper" looked far from tempting. Accordingly, I set out in search of food elsewhere. But, though at regular meal hours a man may stuff himself to his heart's content, after midnight not a scrap is obtainable. Returning to the hotel of the "sleeper," I succeeded in drumming up a Negro in charge of the dining room, who kindly attended to my wants. I rolled one bed against the door and, after saying my prayers—a thing never so far neglected—went to sleep in another.

On waking, I arrived at the sage decision to de-camp. It would have been impossible to give that caravansary as my address. After tramping all over Washington, I at length discovered a hotel called Metropolitan, where they promised that I could have a room at 4 P.M. There is only a single bed there, so that I can be pretty certain they will not attempt to foist a roommate upon me.

As for the aspect of the city, here is a first impression: a long avenue, straight and very broad, connects White House and Capitol. The effect, I must say, is exceedingly fine. Situated on a considerable eminence which dominates the city, the Capitol is truly monumental. From the central mass of the great building rises a vast cupola, resembling our church of the Assumption as to form but much higher and more happily proportioned. This immense dome crowns the central construction, which is flanked by two wings; the Northern wing is the domain of the Senate, the Southern belongs to the House of Representatives, or Congress. If I dared hazard architectural criticism, I might say that the lines are rather rigid and not followed out with sufficient harmony, but the whole effect is grandiose and the view from it sublime.

Looking townward, I see the reaches of the Potomac whose name the events of this war will render immortal. Further, extend the hills which dominate Mount Vernon. At my feet, immense military encampments stretch as far as the eye can see. These have sprung up like mushrooms at the call of necessity. Turning back to the Capitol, I confess that I am deeply moved. From this historic roof issued those edicts which transformed four million oppressed human beings into men and brothers.

My visit began with the Senate, as the session was about to begin. The large square hall where the debates take place is not at all like our *Corps Législatif*.

In the first place, the galleries here can seat a thousand persons and are open to the public except for a relatively small space reserved for the use of foreign envoys and American cabinet ministers. The *Floor,* as they call it, is unlike our *Corps Législatif* in that it is not crescent-shaped with fixed benches or armchairs. The seats, placed in a semi-circle, are three rows deep. A large number of them, abandoned by the Confederates when they seceded from the Union, is kept vacant. A sad sight, these rows whose emptiness, however, marks a hope for the occupants' eventual return.

The President or *Speaker*, who serves as Vice- President of the Republic, is seated on a large armchair elevated somewhat above the rest. His place corresponds to the one in which we saw M. Rouher presiding over our *Corps Législatif*. The clerks of the Senate are ranged on a bench below.

The session opened with a prayer offered by the chaplain who, on such occasions, occupies the Speaker's place. Some of the Senators remain standing until he concludes. The questions I heard debated were not important but the arguments were ably sustained, without the smallest oratorical effort or affectation of speech. They talk simply and as though discussing ordinary business matters. Their appearance is distinguished and intelligent. I left with the impression that the affairs here transacted are well and wisely carried out.

Afterwards, I crossed over to the House of Representatives, which is much larger than the Senate House but disposed in the same fashion. To the right of the Speaker is a panel, framing a bad portrait of Washington. To the left, hangs that of M. de La Fayette by Scheffer. I was glad to see this picture again, for it reminded me of the day when you showed it to me for the first time. It is more effective here than at Beaufossé[1] because placed at a greater distance.

As to the appearance of the House, I do not agree with M. de Tocqueville when he calls it "an impossible assembly, both in appearance and behavior." True, the members are less experienced than are the Senators. They are elected for two years only and change often; but the Assembly presents a good appearance and has nothing savoring of vulgarity. The only reproach that can justly be made is that none of the congressmen has yet become celebrated—that is all.

This brings me to a more important question from the Constitutional point of view: election by second degree. I believe Tocqueville greatly exaggerates the

---

[1] The painting referred to is the original sketch, of which Scheffer made two full-length replicas. One hangs at La Grange, Lafayette's former residence, now in the hands of the Marquis de Lasteyrie. The other is the one belonging to Congress.

mistake of choosing the Senate through nominations by the State Legislature. I think myself that were they chosen directly by the people nothing would really be changed in the composition of this body.

The importance of the Senate consists in the quality of the affairs administered, and all Americans know that important affairs can only be adequately administered by eminent men.

I set forth after dinner to call on M. de Gheraldt, the Prussian Minister, one of the most highly considered persons hereabout. He lives terribly far off in Georgetown. As bad luck would have it, he was not at home, so I shall have to repeat the proceeding.

Mr. Sumner, President of the Senatorial Foreign Affairs Committee, to whom I have several letters besides the one your father gave me, is a very high and mighty personage and seems, at present, in great favor. I am impatient to meet him because I depend on his help to have access to Mr. Lincoln. I have been warned that, should I apply to anyone else, he would be offended. I must also try to see four other Federal Government ministers to whom I have been given letters.

I forgot, in describing the Capitol, to tell you about a small round room completely covered with paintings which record great national events: the Declaration of Independence, the Battle of Saratoga and other victories. Artistically, they are beneath contempt, being comparable to our Salon of Rejected Canvases. One is an execrable portrait of General Grant. Another represents Mr. Lincoln reading the Emancipation Proclamation to his assembled Cabinet in 1862.[1] Never before has an act of the Chief Executive been thus immortalized; neither has anyone dreamed of placing the portrait of a general who is still living in an official building. Such things are usually left to posterity. I cannot believe, though, that the country is in danger of falling under military dictatorship. This is inconceivable, in view of American principles and habits of thought. Neither Grant nor Sherman, I am convinced, ever contemplated such an idea. What does seem certain is that the Central Power and also that of the President will be increased by the present war and that the public will approve this augmentation of power and consequent strengthening of governmental efficiency. But you will probably find such philosophical considerations out of place in this discussion of two execrable paintings.

---

[1] F. B. Carpenter, who executed this large historical painting, studied each personage who figures in it during a long summer when he remained as guest of the Lincolns. While observing his principal model he noted the President's comments and anecdotes, and gathered them into a small volume published in 1870, which, as a psychological study and sympathetic divination of Lincoln's thoughts and feelings, remains of permanent value:—*Six Months at the White House.*

February 23rd

I am settled here fairly comfortably, not so well though as at the Clarendon Hotel in New York. There is a constant coming and going—about fifty arrivals, and as many departures, daily. However, I may say that no second-rate hotel in France could grapple so effectively with such a hodge-podge as is found in this establishment: Army and Marine officers, private soldiers, sightseers, adventurers and legislators. Such a hostelry in Paris would be uninhabitable, a veritable pandemonium. Here, however, complete order reigns. Rules and regulations which are imposed by general consent are infinitely more severe than any hotel-keeper would dare insist upon. Sunday is much more respected than in New York, and the hours for meals are different. Breakfast from seven to ten. Dinner from two to four.

I have not yet given you my impressions of the numerous Negroes that surround me here. When I saw five or six of them clustered round my table for the first time, I confess I felt startled at the sight of so many black hands. I am already used to it now and ready to admit that they are wonderful waiters, in their desire to please infinitely preferable to the New York Irish. They try hard to guess what you may want. Yesterday evening, I asked for a cup of tea. My delighted waiter immediately inquired, "What else?" and was bitterly disappointed when I said: "Nothing else." "That's not right," he replied, and rushed off, bringing back a large tray with four dishes of assorted viands. I had a great deal of trouble explaining that I should certainly not eat them and, when I arose from the table, he was convinced either that I must be very ill or else would shortly die of starvation. I think, nevertheless, that they require more explanations than do their Irish brethren. I did not realize that they could be handsome, but there are many fine-looking mulattoes, tall, slender, perfectly modeled.

This is their gala day, for the House of Representatives has just chosen a Negro chaplain, whose sermons are greeted with much applause. A Democratic news-sheet declared that George Washington would have blushed at such a spectacle—in this I cannot agree. It is certain that the race is now in high favor.

I think it was an excellent idea to let them enlist as soldiers. Equality among men in uniform is the first difficult step. Nothing is better for bringing men together than to live, fight, conquer and die side by side. Thus far it must be acknowledged that they have fought well; fire has not spared them and they have stood up to it bravely.

If you want to understand the growth of anti-

17

slavery sentiment in the North, it must be remembered that every time a billion was spent the cry went up: "If we suppress slavery, it will compensate us for all the pecuniary sacrifices we have made." Now that they have been obliged to spend over twelve billions, the Northerners become more and more radical on the question of slavery. Expenses and abolitionist feeling march side by side. Success is now assured. Each day, new catastrophes fall on the Confederates: abolitionism is at its peak.

In truth, there are now no more slaves in America and the rôle of the apostles of abolitionism has been taken from them; their occupation is gone. So this question naturally arises: Will there be more difficulty in maintaining order in the heterogeneous society which must result from this sudden emancipation? In a political world where Christian sentiment cannot be said to rule, there must be harsh regulations to keep people in order. In default of the Bible, a policeman is indispensable. If political liberty exists to so large a degree in America, it comes from the fact that everybody wants it.

Personally, I assure you, I have been very good indeed, never omit to say my prayers and go to Mass regularly; but, as to abstinence on Friday, that is materially impossible under conditions here.

February 24th

I went to the Senate in order to make an appointment with Mr. Sumner; having done so, we met this morning. The conversation was most interesting and even illuminating. I succeeded in keeping him to the point I came to discuss. His chief defect is a tendency to shy off and pass with ease and elegance from one subject to another, avoiding the main issue. I had been warned of this habit, so I applied myself to bringing my man back mercilessly to the starting place. This afternoon he is going to introduce me to some of his senatorial associates. The day after tomorrow, he hopes to present me to Mr. Seward and to Mr. Lincoln. He treated the subject of Mexico with extreme coldness but seems moderate and anxious to avoid complications; however, he is ready to guarantee that no invasion into Mexican territory will be contemplated. He admits, though, that trouble might arise in case certain rowdy elements should get out of hand. I could obtain no assurance that America would be willing to recognize the claims of imperial France. I was not mistaken in supposing that I must address myself elsewhere to obtain that assurance. The rest of our talk was taken up with mere banalities.

February 27th

So much has happened since my last letter that I must recount events in order. I have been to call on many dignitaries for whom I had letters. Everyone has received me with extreme kindness, vying with one another to instruct or amuse me. On Friday I went to the Senate, where Sumner had invited me to inspect the Library. When I sent in my card, he took me almost forcibly by the arm and led me onto the *floor*, the sacred floor of the Senate. It seems he did the same thing for the Comte de Paris. He wishes me to communicate some of his speeches to certain Paris newspapers. He is most anxious to create a favorable opinion in Europe, in which desire he is perfectly right. So I came home that day at four o'clock and worked far into the night making notes and translations.

The happenings on Saturday were far more sensational. I went to see a certain Mr. Kennedy, director of the Census, a man of distinction who, through correspondence, is well acquainted with Gustave de Beaumont. He does not speak a single word of French but seems to have taken a great fancy to me at first sight and arranged to take me through all the services of the Ministry of the Interior. He introduced me to the under-secretaries. These, in turn, presented me to their chief. Mr. Kennedy told me that Mrs. Lincoln was receiving and that, if I wished, we might go together. This embarrassed me very much for I feared it might offend Mr. Sumner, who reserves to himself this high office, but my new friend argued that this did not matter and would not conflict at all, because it was not the President who would be receiving but Mrs. Lincoln. In brief, I accepted, dressed and started out for the White House. That was Saturday, February 25th, at three o'clock.

The reception was almost over. Many guests had already left. In we went. Upon entering the first parlor, I at once perceived a tall man standing near the door, surrounded by an atmosphere of great respect. No mistake was possible; it was Mr. Lincoln himself! Apparently, when there are so many visitors in Washington, as is now the case on account of the Union victories, the President is apt to come to his wife's receptions. What an anxious moment! Here I was alone, without anyone to help, obliged to say a polite word in English to each of them. No possibility of retreat, though. I had time, while waiting my turn, to observe Mr. Lincoln closely. He is exceedingly thin, not so very tall. His face denotes an immense force of resistance and extreme melancholy.[1]

---

[1] In describing Lincoln's sittings F. B. Carpenter wrote: "Absorbed in his papers, he would often become unconscious of my presence while I studied each line and expression of that furrowed face, the

It is plain that this man has suffered deeply. His eyes are superb, large and with a very profound expression when he fixes them on you. It cannot be said that he is awkward; his simplicity is too great for that. He has no pretense to having worldly ways and is unused to society, but there is nothing shocking in this, quite the contrary. The elevation of his mind is too evident; his heroic sentiments are so apparent that one thinks of nothing else. Nobody could be less of a parvenu. As President of a mighty nation, he remains just the same as he must have appeared while felling trees in Illinois. But I must add that he dominates everyone present and maintains his exalted position without the slightest effort.

I waited fifteen minutes before Mr. Kennedy could bring me up to him and then managed to say that my whole heart was engaged on the side of his political ideals; that I participated enthusiastically in his present success and that of his armies, feeling, as I did, that Union victory was the victory of all mankind. This seemed to please him, for he took my hand in both of his as he said how glad he was to find his policies so well understood.

At the center of another circle, and some steps off

---

saddest face in repose I ever knew. There were days when I could scarcely look at him without crying."—*Six Months at the White House.*

from her husband, stood Mrs. Lincoln. I made her a low obeisance and said that as Mr. Kennedy had associated my name with that of La Fayette she would easily understand how greatly I rejoiced in the success of Mr. Lincoln and the United States of which, at heart at least, I felt myself a citizen. She seemed to understand my English very well and looked pleased at what I tried to express and, as was proved later, she must have attached importance to it.

In height and figure, she reminded me of Madame Pierre de Ségur but with this difference: she must have been pretty when young. She wore an ample silk gown. You have one very much like it. Not a single necklace, only a bracelet.

From there, we went into the third parlor, where a regimental band was installed. A little conservatory nearby, which Mrs. Lincoln herself takes care of, is simple and unpretentious like the rest.

I must say that her receptions, which everybody attends and where toilettes are exceedingly simple, partake of the general atmosphere which reigns in the White House. Guests are imbued with a sentiment of respectful deference toward the occupants of the dwelling. The master himself, if necessary, would be well able to impose this attitude. From what I am told, this dignified atmosphere is quite different from that which surrounded his predecessors.

On emerging from the White House, Mr. Kennedy took me to his own dwelling in order to fetch one of his two daughters with us to a large reception at Mrs. Sprague's, wife of the Senator of that name and daughter of Mr. Chase, former head of the Treasury Department and now Chief Justice of the Supreme Court. This mansion is the finest in Washington and Mrs. Sprague has a reputation for wit and beauty which the Washington ladies are rather impatient of, as I myself was able to observe.

We waited for Miss Kennedy while smoking our cigars. The young lady came in, dressed as for a ball. She speaks a little French. I asked her what sort of reception this would be. It was a large ball. This was hard to believe, as it was about four o'clock! But Mrs. Sprague, not wishing to have dancing on Sunday, had darkened the house as if it were already night, a custom which they tell me is current all over America. Fortunately, I had a white tie.

The whole of Washington society was there. High-ranking officers, cabinet ministers, etc., etc. I was presented to all those whom it might be interesting for me to know. There was a young naval officer, who danced frantically and who never left the side of a pretty girl in a rose-colored dress with whom he seemed on the best of terms. This young man, about twenty-two years old, was no other than Lieutenant

Cushing, who, last week, forced the passage of Fort Anderson and showed, on this occasion, extraordinary audacity and courage.[1] All the newspapers celebrated Cushing's gallant exploit and I felt that I must tell him that his bravery was equaled only by the fidelity of his devotion. But he was so entranced by the rose-colored damsel that he scarcely answered.

The only thing which I could not admire was the supper. The dining room was so small that it was difficult to get near the sideboard, and quite impossible for the ladies to do so. The men were obliged to bring them their food, all naturally on the same plate after the custom of the country. I rendered this service to two ladies but, for myself, thought it would be simpler to wait until I got home. Besides, my appetite was not tempted by this way of serving supper. Except for this detail, I must say that it would be impossible to find more elegant and correct society, where so many distinguished officers and handsome men of excellent manners were gathered. Among them were many already illustrious but their simplicity was notable.

Mr. Stanton, Minister of War, told me that Sher-

---

[1] This was not Lieutenant Cushing's only heroic feat; he blew up the formidable ram *Albemarle* in the Roanoke River by affixing a torpedo to her side from the small skiff he utilized. This boat naturally was dragged under when the ram sunk and the intrepid sailor escaped by swimming.

man must, at this very moment, be marching on Richmond, that he would not linger in North Carolina but would merely go through the State. I asked him how many men were under his command, but it seemed that he did not care to listen to this question. Everyone says that he disposes of 80,000 men.

I received an invitation to visit, with a few others, the Army of the Potomac. Naturally, I accepted. We shall leave in about ten days, as soon as the Congress adjourns. I have heard several very touching things about General Grant. Evidently everyone considers that the great military figure who emerges superlatively from this war is not Grant but his lieutenant, Sherman. It is he who seems to have the sacred spark. Well! Far from being jealous of him, in both their public and private relations, Grant never misses an opportunity to express his most profound admiration for Sherman, often saying: "It is he who should be in command." Nor is this an affected modesty. It seems that he is charmingly sincere on this point.

As to Sherman, they tell me that when he arrived in Savannah, after having traversed Georgia, he telegraphed immediately to the Minister of War: "I am certain now to cross the two Carolinas." They had faith in him and in his assertions, which was a good thing.

Yesterday, I passed several hours with Mr. Sumner. He is so constantly occupied that I have to arrange to slip into his office whenever possible.

A Senator's life just now is really one of hard labor. He goes to the Senate at noon and only gets back at midnight or one o'clock in the morning. We conversed a long time and went into many questions; this means that, for me, the talk is very fatiguing. He has a real need for general conversation, which is irritating to an interlocutor seeking concision. Besides, his opinions are so radical that they are far in advance of actual possibility; revolution, confiscation, violent means of every sort, forced expropriation of slave-holders, everything appears to him legitimate and necessary in order to arrive at his objective. It is the method of the French "conventionnels" and he is just as convinced as they were. Don't tell your father that he is a profound admirer of Garibaldi and of the evildoer, Cavour. In this he reveals the feelings of pride and independence characteristic of certain Americans. Otherwise, he is very intelligent and he is extremely powerful at this moment, although his power is often disputed and even passionately contested.

His private life is full of the same sectarian spirit. There is something very harsh in his make-up. A fair lady told me that Sumner had never even thought of marrying, though his good looks had caused many a feminine heart to flutter. He never allowed himself to be—I will not say seduced—but even to be touched thereby. He is a sort of monk, who remains apart from worldly things. He is centered in the cause he upholds and in his own ambition.[1] This does not astonish me. There is something strange and moving in the way this man, who has recourse to the most violent means in order to accomplish his task, exercises his temporary influence in the midst of the most violent tempests and apparently enjoys braving them. Any opposition to his principles constitutes for him "moral turpitude" and he hates turpitude as God detests sin; so he sets out to chastise the sinner just as God might be supposed to do. He substitutes for eternal flames—of which he cannot dispose—the violence he is past master of. Evidently this American race, and he in particular, has contributed much toward bringing about the rebellion, but he seems just now to have found compensation in the vengeance which he hopes to visit on the enemy.

His influence will be short-lived. It is impossible that he should not wane in power the day that this crisis is over, but, to use his own expression, he still dominates his colleagues because *he has principles*. I may add that he is always charming to me and in-

---

[1] Nevertheless, Sumner fell a victim to the charms of a pretty widow, Mrs. Alice Mason Hooper, but was obliged to divorce her within a year.

variably behaves like a man who is thoroughly well-bred.

I see that my sojourn here has been fruitful and is much more useful than was my stay in New York. I have written there to have your letters forwarded. What a joy to read them! Even the sight of the paper on which you write, dear soul, comforts me.

In the midst of my solitude, which is always agitated and occupied by work, I am never really lonely. I feel that I am near you. Kiss Thérèse for me as hard as I do you with all my soul. When I think that they are still discussing in Europe whether or not the North will subjugate the South, I cannot really believe such folly exists and think I must be dreaming. There is no question but that Sherman is the hero of the hour. His popularity is immense. I should need at least two pages to explain in what this popularity consists. Sunday I shall do so.

March 7th

To continue the thread of my narrative, I am now acquainted with nearly all the important persons in Washington. I still have letters to three or four who are considered notables. I, myself, have been exhibited to many people, who talk politics with friendly frankness. I am everywhere treated as a warm friend who

thinks as they do and with whom explanations are unnecessary. This is not at all the case with our Legation.
Impossible to dream of a situation more foolish than
theirs or one more impolitic. These gentlemen live
among themselves, see nobody, and never speak to any
native. They loudly proclaim that France made only
one mistake, which is not to have immediately recognized the South and, if necessary, declared war on
North America. As a commentary, they add that
Americans are ill-bred, the women badly dressed and
what not. All this is said so publicly that it comes
back to me from all sides at once. You can judge of
the effect which this produces.

Yesterday evening, a big ball which I was obliged to
attend was given at our Legation. All Washington
society was invited, mixed with hoi polloi. I found
Mr. Seward there. As Secretary of State he is by far
the most important man in the Cabinet. On seeing
me, he came over to talk for a while. This took place
at the foot of the platform which had been erected
for the President and Mrs. Lincoln. The French
Legation was grouped beside me and, having noticed
that I had been standing with Mr. Seward, one of my
fellow countrymen said: "Don't you think that Seward
is horribly vulgar?" "No, he is a man with lots of
finesse and extremely amiable, at least to me," I replied. "I must confess that to us he is never anything

but impertinent," retorted my compatriot. Our dialogue stopped there, but, in truth, the explanation is easy. Our Frenchmen criticize everything they can think of and talk perpetually against this country and its government. Seward surely knows this; he is sufficiently astute to divine their sentiments and they take his sharp answers as superb impertinence. He loses no occasion, big or little, to be disagreeable, but certainly they well deserve it.

Political society is rather inclined to appear parvenu. Their present triumphs are the first great successes obtained since the Declaration of Independence. Even the Revolutionary War was child's play in comparison with this terrible duel now being fought to the death. Public sentiment is much excited and very irascible. This is highly comprehensible. One must allow them to be complacent as they enumerate their immense resources, their military strength, their six-hundred-and-fifty war vessels created during four years. This gives them great satisfaction and surely their joy, which appears rather naive, is legitimate and justified by the sacrifices everyone has made. This year, the budget of receipts is more than brilliant and, in order to attain this figure, no one hesitates to accept enormous taxes. Every American gives directly or indirectly the fifth part of his revenue to the State. At the same time, conscription is resorted to several times a year and causes great hardship. All this is borne without complaint, without the slightest murmur. "It is necessary" is the answer. For this reason, in my opinion, the moment is badly chosen for making fun of them. God knows what complaints were heard in France between 1812 and 1814 against Napoleon's levies! In America, they are accepted. The country itself imposes them of its own free will and public feeling brushes aside the very thought of complaint.

I happened to meet Admiral Farragut, the man who took New Orleans, passing against impossible odds, through the cross-fire of the forts, the man who, commanding five vessels, allowed himself to be carried by the current of the Mississippi under the mouths of the Vicksburg cannon, the man who, on board the first of his vessels, negotiated the perilous channel and, by this prodigious act, determined the fall of the fortress. He is a small thick-set man, with strongly marked features which denote immense energy. He is also simple, kindly and good-natured. Having lived some time in New Orleans, he has the pretension of knowing a few words of French; but, frankly, I should not offer him a professorship in our literature. He was anxious to show me just how he had achieved victory, so that I was obliged to take infinite pains in order to help him in his explanations and I am still in doubt whether I understand exactly what means he employed to cover himself with glory.

During these past days, I have seen a good many officers belonging to various staffs; in general, they are distinguished and amiable. They seem all to be enamored of a young lady to whom everybody makes love and whom they all wish to marry. Unmarried girls have every liberty in this country; the married women very little. It is a question of custom. Thus a young girl can very well be out alone or with a cavalier for a whole night when there is a ball. She pays no more attention to her parents than if they did not exist; but every young girl here knows very well how to defend herself. Moreover, she risks very little among the men with whom she has to do. For you must remember America is a country which was almost created by Puritans and public manners are strongly impressed with the iron stamp of severity. Corruption may be found in great centers such as New York but hardly touches the country as a whole.

I said that at this ball there was a platform destined for the President and Mrs. Lincoln. At ten o'clock precisely, the crowd suddenly lined up in two rows, dancing was stopped and the ballroom broke into applause. Mr. Lincoln appeared. He had offered his arm to Mrs. Seward; behind them Mr. Sumner offered his to Mrs. Lincoln. Abolitionism victorious thus made its entry together with the great force which had annihilated the enemy. It seems that this was the first time that such a thing had been seen. The President and his wife took their places on the platform, with Mr. Sumner and Mr. Seward beside them. Then the guests, officers, functionaries, diplomats and so forth began to crowd about in order to present their respects to the established power. This scene lasted until the departure of Mr. Lincoln—that is, for two hours.

This evening I dine with the Prussian Minister and Sumner, after which we are going to pass an informal evening at the White House. The Prussian Minister (Mr. de Gheraldt) is dean of the Diplomatic Corps. He receives the confidences of most of the statesmen here and no one feels obliged to be careful with him, because he is intimate with everybody. As bad luck would have it, this excellent man had been Prussian Minister to Mexico for a long while and is unshakably convinced that the throne of Maximilian is tottering and that his tree has no roots at all. He told me himself that he had recently had a long talk with Mr. Seward in order to prove to him how fragile was our French tenure and added: "I think I convinced Mr. Seward." I believe I have really begun to know the country pretty well and if, in Paris, they had any sense I might make myself useful to them. Passing to quite another subject, I must tell you, in detail, about the Inauguration of the President, to which I was invited on March 4th.

On that day, at eleven o'clock, under a drenching rain, which fell constantly, I followed the crowd and took up my station at the Capitol for the great ceremony. The Inauguration of the President—as it is called—consists in his taking the oath and comprises two distinct phases. The first takes place in the Senate House, the second before the assembled people.

As I was among the small number invited to witness both parts of the ceremony, I shall describe each in turn. Furnished with a special ticket giving access to the *floor*, I pushed with some difficulty through the crowd which besieged all doors and penetrated at last into the Senate chamber. The galleries that day were reserved for ladies who had passes—a good measure, as it prevents too many from occupying this restricted space. There always have to be a few privileged people and, certainly, there is less inequality shown in a favor which is accorded to ladies only. At the moment of my entrance onto the floor, the deliberation still continued uninterrupted. It had gone on for a whole day and night. The assembly had but three-quarters of an hour more of life.

It finally succumbed under the weight of weariness. The noise which became louder and louder in the tribunes made discussion impossible. At a quarter to twelve, the Vice-President, who was about to quit his functions, rose and bade farewell to the assembly in a few solemn and well-chosen words. Whereupon his successor, Mr. Andrew Johnson, sprang to his feet, took immediate possession of the chair and launched into a detestable discourse pronounced in a still more detestable manner which, to the honor of public taste, impressed the auditors most unfavorably.

Mr. Johnson is a self-made man. At the age of twenty, he was a tailor's apprentice and scarcely knew how to read, but, by dint of hard work and natural aptitude, he became successful in politics and entered the State legislature of Tennessee. In 1859 he was elected Senator and with passionate eloquence denounced the then all-powerful slave-masters. On the eve of Secession, he ferociously attacked Jefferson Davis, presidential nominee of the Confederate States. Johnson, although a son of Tennessee, remained unswerving in allegiance to the Federal Government, and this inflexible attitude caused his name to be placed on the electoral ticket of the Union. It seems, however, that during a long period, when out of office, he acquired the wretched habit of drinking to excess and that, when he took over his new functions, he was intoxicated. He was still wearying the assembly with desultory discourse when President Lincoln entered through a door directly facing the Speaker. The Chief

Executive was respectfully saluted by all as he passed along. His bearing was modest. He walked with eyes inclined downward and took his seat in an armchair contiguous to, but below the bench occupied by the Senate clerks. He was dressed in black from head to foot and wore a plain frock coat. During Mr. Johnson's continued ramblings, the President closed his eyes and seemed to retire into himself as though beset by melancholy reflections and totally ignored the many eyes which sought his own in the hope or perhaps expectation of some smile, nod or other sign of recognition on his part, while he, as overcome by the august solemnity of the occasion, remained absorbed.

I had not fully comprehended up to this moment his attitude of selfless modesty, nor conceived that such an exalted position could be sustained with so much religious feeling.

During the few minutes necessary for the Vice-President and the newly elected Senators to take the oath, the floor had filled up. The Chief Justice and members of the Supreme Court, the diplomatic corps, all the representatives of the lower house were there. At this moment, the cortege began moving toward the platform where the President speaks to the people before himself being sworn in. The President headed the procession, still accompanied by the ballot committee which was there to represent the people. Then came Mr. Salmon P. Chase, Chief Justice of the United States Supreme Court who, as the Constitution requires, must administer and accept the presidential oath of office. Then, pell-mell, Senate, Supreme Court, Congress and diplomatic corps follow. I was, thanks to Mr. Sumner, in the first group. I could not help feeling embarrassed at occupying such an honored place.

In order for you to understand the scene I am about to describe, I must give an idea of the stage setting. The main façade of the Capitol looks eastward. The building, which is reached by a long flight of steps, stands very high. On the day of the Inauguration, these stairs are covered and transformed into an immense platform which overlooks the lawn and garden surrounding the Capitol. In the middle of this greenery stands the celebrated statue of Washington, the pedestal of which bears the inscription: "First in peace, first in war, first in the hearts of his countrymen."

The President therefore finds himself just above the crowd, which occupies the entire space, garden, lawn and avenues facing the monument of the father of the Republic. But to return to my narrative, the President issued alone from the Capitol, whereupon a thunder of shouts, hand-clappings and wild hurrahs rent the air. Arm-in-arm with Mr. Sumner, I followed at a very short distance and advanced up to the edge of the platform. The grandeur of the spectacle before me was indescribable.

Beneath, the massed crowd remained respectfully silent, or suddenly broke out into bursts of enthusiasm. Thousands of colored folk, heretofore excluded from such reunions, were mingled for the first time with the white spectators. Further off, to right and left, infantry troops were drawn up. Among them was a Negro battalion. Many uniforms were also distinguishable in the crowd. The sky appeared propitious; a radiant sun had put the mists to flight.

Mr. Lincoln advanced to the edge of the terrace and pronounced an admirable address, which I would translate for you were it not that the newspapers will bring it by the same mail as this letter. For the first time in a presidential speech, slavery is officially condemned.

Frequent applause broke out during the reading, especially at those passages which referred to the abolition of slavery. The speech ended, the President took the oath of office. Chief Justice Chase approached him, holding the Constitution of the United States in his hand, from which he read the article ordaining the taking of this oath. He then addressed the sacramental words to the President. The phrase escaped my ear, but, in a few moments, I saw Mr. Lincoln bow his head and extend his right arm. I can swear that those who witnessed this act were convinced that never was an oath spoken more certain of being kept inviolate.

I am writing to your father at the Vatican but I can only repeat what I have just told you.

March 10th

My life here is divided between study, work and worldliness. For three nights in succession I have come home at one or two in the morning, but what would you have? Add that all my conversation is necessarily in English. To speak is not so hard, but to understand is another matter. Often I find myself thoroughly worn out. Otherwise I am well, have good appetite and feel very energetic. I much enjoy the variety of sights and people.

Yesterday I assisted at a curious and rather melancholy gathering. A dozen Indians, chiefs of their respective tribes, had come to pay their respects to the Government. The authorities here encourage such visits and the Indians themselves, when not too savage, are glad enough to show themselves off. They are lodged by the Government, which gives them presents: necklaces and beads. Also, when requested, they are given agricultural implements and other useful things. I was at the official reception. The evening before,

I had met the high chief of the Chippewas, with his interpreter. The chief, who is intelligent, was delighted to encounter a Frenchman, for we are still popular among them. Canadian history is remembered yet in their tribes. This remark is necessary to the comprehension of the following anecdote. At the Patent Office, where Indian affairs are administered, the door opened and ten or fifteen persons entered dressed Lord knows how! Feathers of all colors and sizes decked their heads; moccasins encased their feet, but, as to clothing, nothing but a red blanket like my own traveling rug. They are tattooed and striped all over, quite pitiful to see, and what is worse, those who wear European clothes are completely grotesque. One of them appeared in an old suit of livery which he wore with laughable gravity.

The room was crowded with curiosity seekers. I asked the Secretary of State whether these Indians found our being there unpleasant. "On the contrary," he replied, "they are delighted to see us." In fact, the first of them came up with a compliment, addressed to the Commission, which the interpreter rendered as follows: "I am enchanted to see our white brothers, who came here by sea; I love these brothers"—adding phrases such as we read in Fenimore Cooper's novels. The three that followed were funnier or perhaps more intelligent: one declared he would like to kiss all the ladies present but perhaps it would be better to transmit his compliments verbally. Everybody laughed. Fortunately, I did not know any of the women present, otherwise I should have been frightened on their account, but, it seems, without reason. Like caged lions, the red men never go too far! Another had just heard that a white brother from France was present, to whom he would like to talk, and I trembled at the idea of being, in my turn, shown off, for it is best not to be exhibited on these occasions. However, it was not demanded of me. The last Indian to come forward requested implements to cultivate his ground. These unfortunates inspire pity. Proud of their savage independence, believing themselves superior to white men and possessing extraordinary physical vigor, they are constantly driven farther and farther by the tide of white immigration, which eventually swallows them up. Their reservations are invaded, but no force can restrain the torrent which engulfs them. Neither laws nor treaties avail. Only one thing remains for them, which would be to renounce their tribal customs and cultivate the soil.

They remain refractory to a civilized mode of life. The Federal Government, which deals with these questions, is powerless notwithstanding many conscientious attempts to find some practical solution. Fifty years more and this entire race will have practically disappeared. *The last of the Mohicans will be but a memory*. Worse, I am told that Barnum is negotiating in order to exhibit some Indian specimen in his circus —painful reflection. I am also saddened by the thought that the Susquehanna being frozen and communication with New York suspended, I cannot guess when this letter will reach you.

March 16th

I am still trying to find a room in Washington instead of continuing to live at this hotel, although, at last, I have succeeded in making myself pretty comfortable. I should like to move for two reasons: the first being that, in town, rooms are much cheaper; second, during the long meal hours, I almost die of boredom. Imagine a hall as long as the dining room in the Hotel du Louvre in Paris filled with small tables like a restaurant. Each guest occupies one-sixth of a table; about a hundred and fifty eat here at the same time. Never a word is exchanged among the guests; no sound is heard except the clatter of dishes manipulated by dozens of black hands; it is enough to put me to flight if I were not hungry.

At the Club, on the contrary, there is table d'hôte which is less expensive. I should also be with Sumner and other interesting talkers. That is where I should go for meals, having been put up by the Secretary of the Interior, who takes his meals there regularly. Thus my way of life will be greatly improved. What an advantage to have learned some English! Earlier, it would not have been possible.

Here is the story of how I first came to this hotel. It is worth telling, showing, as it does, "what fools these mortals be." At the desk, according to formula, I wrote my name on the register. "Chambrun, Paris." No one paid the slightest attention to me and I was conducted into any old hole, though the price is always the same, whether the room be large or small or whether you take every meal or none, under the roof. Some days later a servant brought me a letter. The superscription listed titles and business. That same evening I was called to the office and thus addressed: "Marquis, please excuse us for making you so uncomfortable. . . . In an hour, we shall be able to give you a much better room; you can't possibly stay where you are now!" Just because he had read my address on an envelope the creature was transformed.

This other story will amuse you too. The day of the Inauguration, as I wrote, I was very near the President on the platform, never thinking that I should have a photograph of myself gratis. But this morning, when passing a photographer's window, I was surprised to see myself pictured in the presidential group, quite recognizable though small. I will send you a copy on the first occasion. You will identify your "pigeon" holding his hat under his chin, as he often does.

Here are my plans for the future. I must stay here for some time longer, for I want to know the men in office better and, at the same time, to study the machinery of government, on which it is essential to accumulate much technical information.

I already foresee how much I can make out of the knowledge I have acquired during this trip, as regards a possible future book. I see plainly the outlines of this book and the manner of treating the subject without in the least conflicting with Tocqueville or going over the same ground as he does in his *American Democracy*. I must limit myself to this: describe the changes which the present war must necessarily make in this country. The first part should describe what the Union had come to before the declaration of war: the false and exaggerated conception of local independence (States Rights), a central power reduced to nothing, the seeds of dissolution contained in such a conception. This portion of the work is full of new views, quite unknown in Europe and unpopular here.

The personal influence of Calhoun in all this is something hitherto unknown, and well worth explaining. Secession was seething in Southern hearts and has been arming itself for twenty-five years. Of this there is ample proof.

The second part will show the transformation effected by war. I do not yet see, as plainly as I envisage the first half, how I shall treat this portion. I do, nevertheless, see the principal points to be brought out, especially as regards the consolidation of central power.

I shall conclude with a picture of the successive emigrations which transform America and shall try to conceive what the future of these newly arrived citizens may be. The immigration movement is prodigious. Not since the times of Alaric and Attila have such masses been set in motion. Six million Europeans have arrived in this country during the last thirty years. Germans and Irish form the major part of these. What sort of men are they? What are their plans and aspirations? What will they do in a land totally new to them? Until now, the descendants of the New England Puritans have largely had the direction of government, and dominate the country where they form almost a directing caste. There is no such thing as a perpetual emigration and I believe their original traits will, on settling down, alter or be absorbed. These things appear to me equally new and of great interest to develop. My conscience sometimes steps in. Have I the right to work for myself while receiving a salary from the French Government? The answer is that I do not abate my zeal in the accomplishment of my mission.

At home they can hardly be satisfied at the way things are going here. It has been decided, after some hesitation, that no new American minister will be sent to Paris. International affairs will continue to be managed as at present. I may add that, at the conclusion of the war, they will be sure to find ways of showing temper and ill-will, at least verbally; be as disagreeable as possible. Seward is, from what I can see, particularly irascible. Foreign relations are practically in his hands. I believe that President Lincoln is perfectly sincere in saying: "I do not know Europe. I attend to America; Seward attends to Europe."

Now Seward is candidate for the next presidential election. His program seems to be based on the Monroe Doctrine. It is certain that no one wants war in Mexico but they will go pretty far to insist on this theory: the entire Continent must be under American control.

It would not take much for Mexico to upset the cart. They must stay quiet and not expel American consuls as they have just done at Matamoras. For this once, America closes her eyes and perhaps will do so again, but not forever. The game is too dangerous for that. Public sentiment cannot be predicted. If suddenly American indignation should be aroused at the expulsion of commercial representatives, things might turn very badly in Mexico.

So far, the Government wishes to avoid armed intervention; I am perfectly certain of this while warning that we cannot be too prudent. French troops must be on the spot, as a necessary preventive against any temptation to interference.

After two hours' talk with the President, Mr. Sumner told me very distinctly that Mr. Lincoln clearly saw that America was in a position which allowed her to speak firmly, and, though desirous of avoiding complications with France, my country had behaved so badly that America's duty was to make France feel this. The Secretary of State spoke in the same terms, and with a visible impatience which he vainly tried to dissemble, with regard to certain minor incidents which have just come up, and because of a certain corsair at present cruising near Ferrol in Spain. This, of course, is very serious. I do not know whether I make myself clear but two things seem to me equally certain: First, international affairs, generally speaking, tend toward peace. Second: America's attitude will certainly be pretty stiff.

Here is a detail not very amusing to you but which may interest your father; it concerns the real origin of the Monroe Doctrine. At the time of the emancipation of the Spanish colonies, Europe was still bound by the guiding principles of the Holy Alliance. In the name of these principles, Spain solicited the return of her overseas possessions. Canning, then English Prime Minister, tried to dodge this request and, in aiming to shelve the theory of nonintervention, was obliged to seek an alternative. He consequently wrote Mr. Monroe, President of the American Republic, to this effect. "You are nowise involved in our Holy Alliance; do us the service of affirming loudly that we cannot intervene in any way, shape or form without wounding American susceptibilities." Monroe without malice took up Canning's suggestion and declared that "to mix in the affairs of the American continent was almost equivalent to an attack on the United States." This expedient allowed Canning to disregard the Spanish demands; but he did not foresee how far his suggestion would lead, nor conceive that it would develop into a veritable doctrine.

Monroe, on his side, subscribed to the idea, little thinking that forty years hence it would acquire the force of a dogma.

March 22nd

How long shall I remain here? What a question, my dear soul! Until I have studied America thoroughly and my book is firmly clear in my head. I want, above all else, to come back to you and to have done with this wandering existence, though I must say I find it fascinating. My eyes open wider and wider on many unsuspected things. But I want to regain my freedom and to lead a quiet life with you in Paris, no matter how modest or how laborious. The Press would be the best opening, and I could easily make an arrangement with one or two important New York dailies. They pay well for a good news column, which would make my name known and, better, give me enough work while allowing me independence. Should that dream become a reality, I shall always be thankful for having been here during these past months. Were you beside me, how different would be a solitude *à deux*.

This morning, I received your letter marked "No. 15." This shows that several are missing. Neither 13 nor yet 14 has come to hand. Evidently the service is defective. When I ask why, the inevitable answer is: "Our country has other things to do than to improve the postal service. We must finish the war." If complaints are made about bad roads and dirty sidewalks, the same response: "Wait till the war is finished." When trains are late and accidents numerous, the reply is invariable. Decidedly, a more patient people could not be found.

I am beginning to comprehend the mechanism of

this Government. I have studied the cog-wheels of each administration and my work progresses daily. I understand how the central power functions. It only remains to form a personal opinion on my observations. What strikes me most is its far-reaching influence. In order to appreciate this, the observer must not be in Europe but on the spot. The Federal Government is now employing nearly a hundred thousand functionaries, either in the financial administration or in the War or Navy Departments. All nominations are in the hands of the President. What is true in civil service applies also to the Army. Regular officers, whatever their grade, generals of brigade or division, even volunteers, are chosen by him. Thus, in the name of the President, who is a civilian and who remains practically inaccessible, those who surround him dispense favors and obtain advancement for their protégés.

The American functionary can easily be recalled and any change in the higher spheres is certain to bring about still greater transformations in the ranks. The French functionary's status is entirely different. Once appointed, he is secure. On this side of the Atlantic, he cannot ever feel safe. He is always watched by comrades above and below and is not free to express his political opinions without risk. It is hard work, not only to find a place but to keep it.

Nobody who is not on the spot can appreciate these and other difficulties. It interested me immensely to acquire this information by force of persuasion. There is a general who obtained advancement because of his moderate views on abolitionism. He is, now that he is following the new trend, rising rapidly. My advice today would be: you have not gone nearly far enough! Humanity is much alike the world over. But each government necessarily obliges its servants to follow their petty ambitions as best they can.

I am wondering whether the time has not come for Mr. Lincoln to make a tremendous hit, politically, through an offer of peace. His armies are everywhere victorious; the Confederates are exhausted and seek means of negotiation; five or six days ago they made new overtures. General Lee approached General Grant with a proposal to this effect. It seems to me that the President should now make an appeal for peace and that Grant should lay his victorious sword on the altar of the nation. I see every advantage for the Republic in such an action; it would show that force is compatible with moderation and would also counterpoise the unlimited ambitions of the radical party, always keen to annihilate the Southern Democrats who, even in defeat, remain proud. Unfortunately, Mr. Lincoln is hemmed in by bitter radicals, who refuse to treat on any consideration. President

Lincoln himself will not be able to give the cease-fire order until victory is complete.

Richmond will be evacuated in a few days. This I know positively. The last poor vestiges of the Confederacy are in full retreat with General Lee's broken army. Henceforward we shall witness a war of extermination. The defeated soldiers are going to be nothing but objects of pity; even the rights of belligerents will be denied them: they are just insurgents! Woe to them when they are treated as such! This epilogue to the great tragic drama ought to be deleted. It would be, I am sure, if only for the honor of this Republic, a wretched ending.

March 24th

The hour of decision has struck. Two days more and the evacuation of Richmond will be an accomplished fact. President Lincoln himself has just gone to the front. He must be on the spot in case of two eventualities: immediate proposals of peace or a desperate attempt on the part of General Lee to withdraw his forces and keep up a running battle. As you know, his army is not entirely surrounded. But where would it go? Certainly not very far, without the tacit permission of the Northern Government. Should the authorities here accede to the rumored proposal, Lee and his men are not only ready but anxious to march on Mexico and effect its conquest. Yes indeed, Mexico! Neither more nor less! If so, here are these pretended Southern friends, whom France and Maximilian considered as ardent supporters, now getting ready to play this dirty trick. A fine example of our clever diplomacy! The French Government mistrusted Lincoln and considered the North inimical; it is now the South, our alleged friend, that is planning such a blow. Today, the North alone can prevent this hostile action.

These are the reasons which determine Mr. Lincoln to visit the storm center himself. He will remain there until Tuesday next, having left yesterday at noon, taking his wife with him.

Sherman continues to march without halting in the direction indicated by my last letters. This uninterrupted advance is the determining cause of the evacuation of Richmond. It is quite possible that the telegraph will bring you simultaneous news of these events. The description of an engagement in which the Southern forces are represented as having been victorious is completely erroneous, as I have taken pains to verify; the Confederates fabricate such legends in order to maintain the morale of their army.

I think that I have now mastered the intricacies of Washington's administration. It is only here, on the spot, that I can study the evolution of a favorite idea of mine. I have always believed that a principal reason for the failure of our free institutions grows out of the weakness of those who in Europe are called the *Parliamentarians*. Their weakness is shown up, over here, in an illuminating manner. The tide of opinion in America finds means of expressing itself with vigor and eloquence and it is only in following what I observe over here that you can possibly understand it in France.

March 27th

The day before yesterday there were violent engagements on the Potomac. More frightful massacres! I cannot bear all this slaughter. Think that a town of five or six thousand souls can be unpeopled in a few hours. What a disaster! And yet everyone here is so accustomed to this butchery that they hardly pay attention! No nation, I believe, fears death less than America. The reason perhaps is that the American soldier views it as his *business*. He remains stoically under fire without yielding an inch, and falls without a whimper. The thinned ranks are constantly filled up and the newcomers retain the same spirit. The soldier, when wounded, makes no complaint and the infantryman rushes forward with unfailing dash to inevitable destruction. The image of death does not here wear the tragic mask older civilizations are accustomed to give it. It takes a people who are still extremely young, with great hope and confidence in their country's future, for this to be possible. But, after such a digression, I must return to the subject.

Along the Potomac, as on Sherman's battle-front, the success of the Northern armies is equally manifest. The end is near. Everyone here believes that the fighting, day before yesterday, was the prelude to Richmond's evacuation.

I can shed few tears on the death of Morny[1] but I cannot help thinking of what a vacancy his going will leave. What will that poor Goddess of Liberty do without him? What will become of that factitious and incomplete freedom, now that her protector is no longer there? American newspapers give little space to all this; European news resolves itself into detailed analyses of English affairs. France plays a minor rôle. The only topics in vogue are the theatre, the fashions and the financial market. England is in a very different situation. To Americans, in spite of

[1] Charles Louis Flahaut, later Duc de Morny, reputed half-brother of Napoleon III, died March 10, 1865. He helped the latter in his coup d'état of December 2, 1851. After that event, he held the office of Minister of the Interior and subsequently became a member of the Legislative body. In 1854—and from that time to the time of his death —he was its president. Though a firm partisan of the Empire, he did not always approve certain dictatorial acts of the regime and passed as having liberal tendencies.

everything, she remains a first cousin. They may not like each other but they still belong to the same family. When you hear the fuss that is made over there about "French thought," I can assure you that a Frenchman like me feels pretty small over here.

I have read a letter from the Comte de Paris[1] and another from Augustin Cochin,[2] both shown me by Mr. Sumner. The one from the Comte de Paris was twenty pages long. It is a very clear and circumstantial report on the state of affairs in America. He thinks as I do about Mexico and I believe that Mr. Forcade is of the same mind, judging from the article I have just read. His views, on the whole, are moderate and interesting, far the best thing from his pen that I have read.

As for Cochin, he covers Sumner with compliments and compares him to Wilberforce. As a matter of fact, the two men are no more alike than Napoleon is like Guizot. These compliments pleased the Senator a great deal, though he apparently found them rather insufficient. Now that the first part of the task he set out to

---

[1] Comte de Paris, 1838-1894, grandson of Louis-Philippe, King of France. Came to America at the beginning of the Civil War and served on McClellan's staff. His book on the Civil War is considered one of the best authorities and is rated very highly in America.

[2] Augustin Cochin, 1823-1872, writer and philosopher, known for his liberal Catholicism. Wrote on the abolition of slavery, a life of Abraham Lincoln and many other works.

do has been accomplished and that the Negroes have become free men, he is tempted to undertake a new effort. First of all, his enemies must be confounded. The proud and unconquerable Southerner must be abased, and made to bite the dust. This project is astonishing, even incomprehensible, to those who view it from afar. On the Northern side, great enthusiasm, enormous energy and an obstinate will to go forward prevails, no matter what sacrifices may ensue. On the Southern, we cannot but admire an incomparable force of resistance. Broken, beaten down to earth, without arms and without credit, a handful of ruined men struggle on with fanatical fury and patrician pride. The very moment they seem lost, they rise up as though moved by an electric spark. Strange phenomenon this indomitable courage which nothing can shatter and which the greatest misfortune cannot bow down!

To return to Mr. Sumner, where can you find in him a particle of the kindly humanity of Wilberforce? This titanic struggle is not that of a polished world. In this world, constructed on pillars which have not yet been rounded off but remain primitive, square and solid, the spiritual conflict involved is almost inconceivable to the French mind.

The question of slavery came up in the midst of all this violence, and when the fight was once feverishly joined, the North suddenly perceived that the whole prosperity of the Southern States was based solely on this institution. Slavery, according to their own declaration, was the cornerstone of their edifice. From this moment, slavery was the thing to be attacked, and the abolitionists, with Sumner at their head, rushed into the arena. As long as the fight was merely to preserve the Union, the Southern adversary was never attacked at his most vulnerable point. His essential interests were not compromised. Sumner utilized this argument with force, but did not at first capture the President's ear. Yet when it became evident that enthusiasm might cool off, if this essential cause were neglected, Mr. Lincoln launched the Emancipation Proclamation in 1862. This was a body-blow to the adversary because it inflamed to white heat the passions of the abolitionists.

Hence the great radical success, Sumner's more particularly. At the very moment when the ardor of the fight was cooling, he came out with a new and decisive element in favor of the North. Having found the chink in the adversary's armor, it was against that vulnerable spot that all his energies were directed. From that time forth, the enthusiasm for abolitionism made giant strides. It is now at its most acute stage. True, radical leaders conducted their campaign ably and their blow was struck with astonishing force; but it is absolutely false to affirm that such a kindly, pious and religious genius as Wilberforce could be party to their extravagances. The radicals took possession of the political stage and, having appealed successfully to the strongest passions, succeeded in dominating their more moderate opponents. I use the term "strongest passions" expressly because the most noble instincts were here inextricably mingled with baseness and cupidity. The same edict which decreed abolition of a most shameful traffic pronounced also the confiscation of property without indemnity to the owner, whose goods were an object of envy. The most odious methods of seizure marred the noblest designs.

As to the Constitutional Amendment, it is a page in history which it is extremely difficult to write: real good and relative good are there combined. Generous intentions motivated many who drew it up, but they were aware at the same time that its draconian severity was excessive.

Yesterday I visited the Navy Yard, which is near my lodgings, and saw what they call a *Monitor*. Imagine a boat entirely constructed of iron, the bulwarks of which are nearly level with the waves. At the center of the deck rises a great black tower, also of iron, eighteen inches thick, large enough to contain two enormous cannon, whose deadly mouths project through window-like apertures. This vessel has already been honorably scarred. Enemy bullets struck her, but without doing other injury than to leave their marks upon her indomitable shell. Nearby rode a splendid corvette built in wood, with high slender masts and snowy rigging—a curious companion for the iron monster, but she follows it everywhere and takes it in tow when the weather is bad. When fighting begins, she remains at a distance while the somber creature accomplishes its work of death. Nothing is more characteristic, it seems to me, of our modern society than the constant effort, to the detriment of beauty, to perfect the *machine* and render destruction quicker and easier.

March 31st

The President is prolonging his visit to the camps. He convoked a war-council Tuesday. This was composed of Grant, Sherman and Sheridan. Today, rumors of peace are again rife. Lee has asked for a parley, so Mr. Seward left at once. The time has come for us to be careful in Mexico. If President Lincoln simply says to Jefferson Davis: "I will shut my eyes when you cross the Mississippi," there are chances that the monarchy of Maximilian will be in a bad fix. Does the American Government understand, I wonder, that they must not try to delegate to the South things that they would never do themselves? This is a delicate question. . . . It is easy to evade it by saying, "the North has done nothing and will do nothing. You have been counting on the South, you French. Very well, then, arrange your affairs with their leaders; if they turn on you, *we are very sorry.*"

Admit that such negotiation fails, still peace cannot be far off. Today from a direct source, I received statistics of the forces engaged. They are terrifying. Grant has a hundred and fifty-five thousand men; Sheridan fifteen thousand cavalry. He has left Danville by rail, in order to cut off communications with Richmond. Sherman has now a hundred and twenty thousand men, not counting cavalry and artillery. General Thomas, with thirty thousand, is on the way from Tennessee to Lynchburg and, to conclude, eighty thousand men are operating in Alabama. I speak only of those who are in action. It is certainly prodigious that any people, after four years of war, should still possess such resources.

Here I see a number of officers, generally of two distinct types: the one, a politician or statesman, who is a kind of radical apostle of the abolitionist faith. This type comprises all those of German origin, whether through family or through emigration. The other is the citizen who has become a soldier because it is a business like any other, as he might, at another time, have become a candlemaker. When his country appealed to him, he responded readily to the call. Meanwhile, he is in a hurry to finish so as to take up another job. He has no great passion for abolitionism. He wants his country to be great, united, to smash the South and return to other business. Generally, this sort of man thinks of establishing himself in the South and starting some kind of enterprise.

When an American has been doing the same thing for many years, he is often disposed to begin something else. Here, out of a thousand, is one striking example; it is that of Sherman himself. After graduating from West Point (Military Academy), and being accustomed to dressing badly, he could not accept either uniform or military discipline. He gave up the profession and left for California, where he became a lawyer. Grant was there also, engaged in legal practice. Afterwards, Sherman became a banker in New York, and failed. He then went to Louisiana, where he accepted the post of Professor of Military Tactics. No doubt he did well and, without suspecting it, instructed in military art a great number of his future adversaries. When war was declared, he was thus engaged, but hurried North at once and, presenting himself to his old California friend, Grant, asked for a command. It was he who laid siege to Vicksburg but proved hardly up to the task. However, Grant took him under his wing, gave him advancement and, when everyone else denied him ability, foresaw his great career. Until the terrible battle known as Chattanooga, Sherman got along, more or less well. After this encounter, where the enemy was badly beaten, Grant, nominated to Supreme Command, made it—much to his honor—a condition of acceptance that the Western Armies should come under the command of Sherman. This was the birthday of Sherman's glory. From that instant, he truly revealed himself, and I, who try to observe events impartially, cannot doubt that, at this very moment, he is writing one of the most brilliant pages in military history.

I have been examining into a situation which is most interesting. There are three Germans here who all occupy very high positions: Sigel, Sedgwick and Schurz. These names sounded familiar and somehow awoke an indistinct memory. After investigation, I learned that all had been active in Germany during the revolution of 1848. They were denounced for subversive doctrines and sent into exile. They chose America as a refuge. Fifteen years sufficed to place them in prominent positions as ardent abolitionists. Having had several occasions to observe their German compatriots here, I am struck by their contentment under the American regime. They are good citizens and loyal to the Government, an example of how men who were stifled in Europe, once having renounced their subversive ideas, find their place and their ideal in the American social system. Professed enemies of order and established institutions, in Prussia or Austria, here they are perfectly quiet and happy, readily giving their intelligence, activity and even their blood in the service of a new country. This is natural enough. To these youthful seekers after Utopia, what was a dream in Europe here becomes a reality.

This brings me to another observation worthy, I think, of a minute's attention: during all the revolutions in Europe, it is noticeable that the leaders aspired to establish ideals which were too advanced for their special country and never reached attainment. The Cromwellian Revolution never satisfied England's extreme Radicals such as Milton, but, on the other side of the Atlantic, what Milton had desired for his own country took root on this soil. For these Germans the situation is reversed. They left their ideas behind them and have been able to conform to American habits. European advanced opinions seem to settle down into normal development under the Federal Government, where the spirit of destruction, once sidetracked, is transformed into creative energy.

Thanks to my constant English reading, I am making great linguistic progress. I have not read one line of French since my arrival in America. Grammatical study and especially constant English conversation have led to this result. No one can believe that I began the language less than three months ago. My principal defect is pronunciation. I have not, up to now, been able to grapple with TH, but I make myself understood on every subject and can even joke in English. Nothing is better than to be forced by necessity into making this effort. There are not ten persons —man or woman—in Washington who speak French. So there is nothing to do but to adopt the tongue of the country.

April 3rd

This morning, at half-past eleven, there was a knock at my door and a fellow-guest burst in, out of breath, to announce the great news: Richmond, already evacuated, has been taken. He was so moved that he literally fell into my arms. We ran downstairs where everything was in a tumult. Sumner lives a few steps away. I found him his cheeks wet with tears. It took but a few moments for Washington to be all excitement. Cannon thundered. Orators seized the occasion for speech-making. Some from a table, some from a window-sill, hastened to preach the necessity of taking immediate advantage of victory. Some recommended the invasion of Mexico and Canada instanter. During the last eight hours the extraordinary spectacle before my eyes has varied in certain details but continued noisily enthusiastic. While I write, whisky, a liquor horribly popular here in America, contributes largely to the expression of the citizen's joy. I can add little to the news, which the telegraph must have given you this morning. After eight days of constant fighting, thirty thousand of Lee's soldiers were *hors de combat*. His communications were cut, his units surrounded. His grievous losses are the most eloquent proof that all this must be brought to a rapid conclusion. He fled from Petersburg, leaving Richmond to his right but with Grant hot on his track.

It seems that two hundred-and-fifty thousand colored troops were drawn up before the city and entered it, summoned by a band of Negroes within. Consequently, Richmond, so long a target for rifle and cannon fire, was taken without a skirmish.

Will Grant succeed in capturing Lee and his entire forces? This is ardently hoped for, without any real reason for believing it likely. The President, however, telegraphed his wife, three days ago, that they expected to take all in one sweep of the dragnet. I hope with all my heart that they may capture the enemy and persuade him to lay down arms. If there is a capitulation, you will readily understand that it will be the end of Mexico. That is certain.

It is to France's interest that the defeat should be definite and that a cease-fire be obtained without parley. Otherwise the South might, in compensation for surrender, demand free entrance into Mexico.

There is another nation, England, whose accounts will be hard to settle. Many complex questions of maritime law are involved. Great Britain has behaved badly toward the Federal Government. She supplied the South with powder, carried by ships which ran the blockade, and furnished the Confederacy with cannon and all kinds of ammunition. Now the time has come for settlement. America's claim amounts to forty million dollars and she warns England to acknowledge indebtedness at once or keep an eye on Canada. The situation there is even more tense than our own, should the solution of the Mexican question not be what I hope.

Mrs. Lincoln has just sent me special permission to traverse the lines of the Federal armies at any point whatever. I may now go where I please and without the slightest trouble. I think I am the only foreigner who has been given this privilege. I may say, without conceit, that I have taken hold here. I am well liked and seem to be considered, almost everywhere, as a sincere friend of the country's cause. They trust me accordingly. I may say, frankly, that I have never failed to deserve this confidence either in speech or writing.

Mr. Lincoln has had, for such a potentate, three very singular days. He was on a boat at City Point, having as companion a single staff officer and as servants only two Negresses. All had left for the firing-line. Grant sent telegraphic reports directly to the President, who transmitted them himself to the War Department in Washington. I met a general today, just arrived, but who left immediately to join Sherman's army. He had seen the President in the above-described situation. When invited by Mr. Lincoln to remain with him for twenty-four hours, he was obliged to decline on the plea that he must go where honor called.

I can never accustom myself to the way Americans take danger. I know several families whose nearest and dearest are in the thickest of it, as they belong to Sheridan's corps. You would hardly think they felt anxious. The thought that a single shell or rifle ball might annihilate what is most precious to them does not seem to cross their minds. It is the same with the men who go to the front. Today I said good-bye to a young fellow leaving for one of the most exposed positions. His room was next mine and I watched him pack his kit. He left nearly all his baggage behind and, each time he put aside an object, he remarked, "All right, I will find that fifteen days hence." The idea that he would be in danger of his life a score of times during those fifteen days apparently did not even enter his head. This is something I can't analyze and which always astonishes me.

Now that the struggle is about to end, the South will be in a terrible state. The last few months have been destructive to an inconceivable degree. The Western Armies were suddenly seized by an unreasoning spirit of vengeance.

The hunt for slaves, under pretense of setting them free, has degenerated into a system of organized pillage; fire adds to the havoc made by the sword. The passage of Sherman's forces has left in its wake a veritable path of destruction. During the French Revolution, they would have merited the name: *"Colonnes Infernales."* If the insurgents do not lay down their arms within a week, hell will break loose.

As I define it now, the war will have had three distinct phases: The fight for and against the Union, which might be called the political phase. The fight against slavery or the phase of social justice. Now, alas! we are entering the phase of revenge.

If the South does not surrender, armies five-hundred-thousand-men-strong will be active on everv front. Woe to those who refuse allegiance to the Union!

Mr. Stanton, Secretary of War, has just told me that, during three and a half years of conflict, the North lost a million men killed in action or who died in hospital or rebel prisons.

The Confederate losses are certainly equally heavy. What a holocaust! Not excessive perhaps when we think of the results accomplished. I am convinced that if the Federals had won the first battles, making the war shorter, slavery would have quietly continued to be practiced. Time was required and many sacrifices were demanded before this triumph.

April 4th

Nothing new since this morning. Grant continues his pursuit; that is all. Will he succeed? There are serious reasons to think so. The President is on the point of making important decisions. Perhaps he may issue a proclamation.

Will it concern the future attitude toward the South or a promise to the Negroes? Mrs. Lincoln is going with Mr. Sumner to the encampment. Both have been bidden there by the President. I can guess what the political reaction will be all over the country: surely, an attempt to root out rebellion definitively. It is a crucial moment.

To my astonishment, Mrs. Lincoln, who is returning to the Army of the Potomac in company with Mr. Sumner, invited me this evening to go with them. I am leaving tomorrow, at ten o'clock, on the President's private steamer. I need hardly tell you not to be worried; considering with whom I go, risks are negligible.

Washington is literally wild with joy. Judging by the papers, this feeling is general throughout the land. Here it is explosively manifested, with a vigor such as I have never before witnessed. Tonight the town is splendidly illuminated, the cheers, shouts and hurrahs are deafening. To those who know what the people have suffered, such outbursts are comprehensible.

We must remember that this is a people's war, that those in power, and the capitalists of New York and elsewhere, have followed the impulsion, not led it. It is the real American who has shed his blood and paid, without murmuring, one-fifth of his revenue in taxes. So much the better if he is satisfied. It would be better still if he did not get drunk. Sumner explains that this is a trait of the South. There alone, according to him, intoxication is really prevalent. I accept his theory for the time being but shall suspend judgment until I have further evidence. I am indeed curious to see whether this vice will disappear when liberty is established.

April 10th

I am just back from the front and, before going to bed, will describe the visit.

As I told you, we left Washington at eleven, Wednesday morning, the guests being Sumner, Mr. Harlan, Minister of the Interior, with his wife and daughter, an Under-Secretary, and myself.

Mrs. Lincoln drove us to the boat, which was waiting, and we started off under full steam. In accordance with our schedule, we went down the Potomac as far as the sea, then turned into Chesapeake Bay and ascended the James River up to City Point, a distance of about 450 kilometers made in twenty-four hours. I had no sensation of seasickness. We arrived Thursday at noon. President Lincoln was on his own steamer, the *River Queen*, a charming and comfortable yacht on which I passed four days.

The President at once showed us the saloon where the celebrated conference of Hampton Roads took place. He indicated his own seat, that of Seward and of the three Southern Commissioners: Stephens, Campbell and Hunter. The President himself is now accompanied by Admiral Potter, commanding the Federal Fleet, a young and energetic-looking sailor whose simplicity of manner and language are characteristic. It was decided to proceed immediately to Richmond. The President, who had been there the day before to inspect this unhappy city, remained behind; so, a few minutes later, we started again up stream.

City Point had been, for eleven months, general headquarters and center of the cantonments for the Southern troops. The town is almost lost in the midst of this vast military agglomeration. But, after describing our visit to the camps, I shall come back to this.

Signs of devastation began almost immediately after leaving. The river is full of wreckage from the vessels which have been blown up; dead horses are scattered all along the banks. *Plurima mortis imago*—just ask the family Latinist to translate this. The greatest care had to be taken, on account of sunken torpedoes lying dormant in the river-bed. These infernal machines explode at first contact. The sights are more formidable on approaching Fort Darling. There the earth has been constantly plowed up. Bastioned forts occupy both sides of the river at regular intervals, three rows deep. The rebel cannon are still there, untouched, as though ready to cross fire upon any daring marauder. The cannoneers, however, are wanting to complete the picture. Instead, a few Federal soldiers may be seen quietly fishing at the foot of these abandoned retrenchments.

Suddenly, on rounding a curve of the river, we came in sight of church steeples. Richmond was before us. A moment later, we tied up at the wharf. A guard was ready to protect us, a useless precaution, carriages were waiting and we hastened to jump in, feeling very chilly about the waist. Not a word was spoken in our party. Hundreds of Negroes, gathered near the boat landing, precipitated themselves upon us. As we passed, they saluted the "Yankees" with loud enthusiasm. At the left was stacked a mass of burned railroad material, at the right, from a long row of houses, smoke and flame were still rising. We proceeded through the streets; on either side all the stores had been pillaged. Blinds were drawn down, shutters tightly closed. Before retreating, the Confederates had released all the convicts in order to set fire to the town. From the doorways, terrified white people peeped out; they darted angry glances toward us, but showed no other sign of hostility. The aristocracy of the place, when they had not already taken flight, remained close within doors. On all the windows the green Venetian blinds were hermetically shut. We arrived at Jefferson Davis' mansion, now Federal Headquarters. General Weitzel, who is in command, showed us through the residence of the ex-

President of the Confederacy, who had carried away everything movable in his hasty flight. But, foreseeing that his house would be used for this purpose, he had instructed the few domestics left on the spot to this effect: "Take good care of the General who will occupy my old home." The mansion was a fine building, with beautiful parlors, but the red velvet furniture was much worn. General Weitzel gave us all the information we could desire. Among other things, he told us that Mrs. Lee, with her two daughters, still remained in Richmond. After this, we went to the State Capitol.

Words cannot describe the condition of the rooms occupied by the Confederate legislature. What dirt and confusion these last days have accumulated there! It recalls nothing human. A Federal court is already installed in another part of the building. We then made a tour of the city, where the most painful sights awaited us. The entire center has been the prey of fire and the ruins are still smoking. Portions of brick walls have fallen and nearly obstruct the streets. Devastation is complete. We stopped at the prisons, now filled with rebel soldiers. Mrs. Lincoln was anxious to see them. Almost all these unfortunates rose respectfully; some few, however, hissed or whistled. There are nine hundred captives here at the moment. When the Confederates were in power, there were as many as three thousand Northerners packed into the same space. On learning of these numbers and noting the small capacity of the building, our indignation overflowed.

It was almost night when we regained the *River Queen*. Nocturnal navigation was pronounced impracticable on account of concealed torpedoes, so it was decided that we would sleep on board.

When darkness fell the spectacle was fearful indeed. The rebels had destroyed the gas tanks and water pipes. It was impossible to find candles in the ravaged shops. The houses were buried in obscurity. No sound of hoofs in the abandoned streets, not a single voice raised in this city of thirty thousand souls. But on the other side of the town, before us, an immense wall of fire rose into the air. I could not help being sorry for the poor inhabitants without anything to eat but salted beef distributed by the Federal supply service, and a few handfuls of cornmeal. Yet not a complaint was heard. To sum up the situation: enthusiasm among nearly all the Negro population, satisfaction among the poor whites, and total eclipse of the land-owning aristocracy.

The following day, at nine, we again found ourselves at City Point and, at noon, on the way to Petersburg, by the railroad which runs at right angles to the river. This time, the President was with us. We grouped ourselves around him in an ordinary day-

77

car; although intended for the President's private use, several officers filtered in without attracting attention. They were not the only intruders; curiosity had also incited several Negro waiters from the *River Queen* to join the party; they were permitted to sit quietly behind us in the same car.

We crossed all the Federal lines, then those of the rebel strongholds. To our left rose Fort Steadman, where only nine days ago five thousand men had met their death. The plowed-up earth was all that remained as witness to this carnage. On nearing Petersburg, the train was obliged to slacken speed; it had hardly been possible to re-lay the track through this mass of ruins. The depot buildings had been torn down and the railroad bridge wrenched asunder.

Petersburg looks less desolate than Richmond, though Federal bullets and shells have scarred many houses. Bridges were burned, rolling stock was destroyed, but the city itself was not set on fire. The President, I must say, was well received. Everyone who approached was graciously saluted and given a cordial handshake.

On Saturday, we visited the wounded and rapidly inspected the hospital camps. What a review! It began at midday. God only knows all its horror. Materially, the installation is fine; nothing is lacking which can alleviate suffering. But, alas! this cannot be eliminated. We passed before all the wounded and amputated. Some had a leg cut off, some an arm. Amid this terrible mass of agony, not a cry nor a complaint. These tents or wooden barracks are installed with every comfort. They are well supplied with newspapers. Each bed has a Bible beside it. Almost all the wounded soldiers asked the President how the fight was progressing and inquired as to the political outlook, then smiled happily when told: "Success all along the line." Many whom I saw, though suffering atrociously, gave no sign; this, not because we were present, but out of personal self-respect.

I will pass over the worst and most painful cases. I would rather consecrate the last lines of my letter to incidents of another sort. An officer who escorted us inquired whether I should like to see the kitchen. On my affirmative answer the doors opened and disclosed a handsome woman, visibly worn out, dressed in blue linen with white apron. I was struck by her style. My escort, with every mark of respect, introduced me to Miss Gilson of Massachusetts. With the manners of a woman of the world, and with most perfect diction, she graciously showed me all the phases of her work. She presides over the selection of the daily regimen and prepares it herself. She sleeps in a little corner, screened off from the kitchen, on a small camp bed—four planks and a thin mattress. The book on a table beside this bed was naturally the Holy Bible. I was so moved that I expressed my admiration in fluent English—although I could not get rid of my accent: "After having been so much impressed by your soldiers' fortitude, may I be allowed to render homage to yours."

As a matter of fact, and, as was explained to me later, this wealthy young lady, who has an excellent position in Boston society, abandoned all in order to consecrate herself to this hard and monotonous life.

Suddenly, from among the wounded I heard a familiar voice calling me. Turning, I saw the same young man I had met at the ball in Washington. His shoulder was fractured by a rifle bullet, but this did not prevent him from being gay. It was Lieutenant Cushing!

The visit to the Sanitary Division concluded, we drove to Headquarters, situated on the far side of the town, in a fine suburban mansion already surrounded with luxuriant Spring vegetation. While Mr. Lincoln conferred with the generals commanding the garrison, we visited the masterless house and the abandoned gardens. These were beautifully laid out. I have forgotten the name of the former owner, which our escort told me, but I remember his harsh, uncompromising comment: "These people were traitors."

On regaining the carriages waiting to take us back

to the train, Mr. Lincoln stopped to admire an exceptionally tall and beautiful tree growing by the roadside and applied himself to defining its particular beauties: powerful trunk, vigorous and harmoniously proportioned branches, which reminded him of the great oaks and beeches under whose shade his youth had been passed. Each different type he compared, in technical detail, to the one before us. His dissertation certainly showed no poetic desire to idealize nature; but if not that of an artist, it denoted extraordinary observation, mastery of descriptive language and absolute precision of mind. At six in the evening we were once more aboard and on our way to Washington. You may be sure that during this trip I made a quantity of notes and observations, being, as I am, the first foreigner and, moreover, the first unofficial civilian who has witnessed these astonishing sights and had the advantage of first-hand explanation or commentary. I intend to set them down and to write a complete article on what I have seen; but that will require time and care, for, if it is ever to appear in a French review, the style must be more careful than when I am just writing to you personally. Please keep it until my return to France.

(At this point the diary is interrupted by a note. My mother writes that the article referred to,

never published in French, was translated for Scribner's Magazine *(9 January, 1893) by her son.*[1] *Being in possession of the full text, I insert here the most interesting paragraphs concerning the visit to Petersburg and the return to Washington.)*

We were to leave City Point on Saturday, April 8th. A few hours previous to departure, a military band from Headquarters came on board the *River Queen*. After they had given us several pieces, Mr. Lincoln thought of the *Marseillaise*, for which he professed great liking, and asked to have it played. The French anthem was performed a second time; while turning toward me, Mr. Lincoln remarked: "You have to come over to America to hear it."[2] He then asked me if I had ever heard the rebel song *Dixie*, to the sound of which all the Southern attacks had been conducted. I replied in the negative. The President continued: "That tune is now Federal property and it is good to show the rebels that, with us in power, they will be free to hear it again." So he told the surprised musicians to play it for us. Thus ended our last evening.

---

[1] Pierre, Marquis de Chambrun.
[2] The *Marseillaise* was proscribed in France during the Second Empire.

At ten o'clock our boat steamed off. Mr. Lincoln stood a long while gazing at the hills, so animated a few days before, now dark and silent. Around us more than a hundred ships at anchor gave visible proof of the country's maritime strength and testified to the great tasks accomplished.

Mr. Lincoln remained absorbed in thought and pursued his meditation long after the quickened speed had removed the lugubrious scene forever from our sight.

On Sunday, April 9th, we were proceeding up the Potomac. That whole day the conversation turned on literary subjects. Mr. Lincoln read aloud to us for several hours. Most of the passages he selected were from Shakespeare, especially *Macbeth*. The lines after the murder of Duncan, when the new king falls a prey to moral torment, were dramatically dwelt on. Now and then he paused to expatiate on how exact a picture Shakespeare here gives of a murderer's mind when, the dark deed achieved, its perpetrator already envies his victim's calm sleep. He read the scene over twice.

Passing before Mount Vernon, I could not help saying: "Mount Vernon, with its memories of Washington, and Springfield, with those of your own home— revolutionary and civil war—will be equally honored in America." As though awakened from a trance, the

President exclaimed: "Springfield, how happy I shall be four years hence to return there in peace and tranquility!"

Our party dispersed on arriving at the Potomac wharf. Mr. and Mrs. Lincoln, Senator Sumner and I drove home in the same carriage. As we drew near Washington, Mrs. Lincoln, who had hitherto remained silently looking at the town, said: "That city is full of enemies." The President, on hearing this, retorted with an impatient gesture: "Enemies, never again must we repeat that word."

When success at last had crowned so many bloody efforts it was impossible to discover in Lincoln any thought of revenge or feeling of bitterness toward the vanquished. His only preoccupation was to recall the Southern States into the Union as soon as possible. When he encountered opposition on this point, when many of those surrounding him insisted on the necessity of strong reprisals, he would exhibit signs of impatience, for though uninfluenced by such opinions, on hearing them, he gave evident signs of a nervous fatigue which he partially controlled but was unable to dissimulate entirely. On one point his mind was irrevocably made up. The policy of pardon, in regard to those who had taken a principal part in the rebellion, appeared to him an absolute necessity. Never did clemency suggest itself more naturally to a victorious chief. We were with him when he received the despatch from General Grant announcing that the final surrender of the whole Army of Virginia could be foreseen and might take place on the 11th or on the 12th. He added: "Perhaps at the same time we can even capture Jefferson Davis and his cabinet." This announcement greatly troubled Mr. Lincoln, who forcibly pointed out the difficulty and embarrassment in which the Government would be placed by this untimely capture.[1] One of those present, who enjoyed perfect freedom of speech, exclaimed: "Don't let him escape. He must be hanged." The President replied very calmly by repeating the phrase he had used in his Inaugural Address: "Let us judge not that we be not judged." Assailed anew by the remark that the sight of Libby prison rendered mercy impossible, he twice repeated the same biblical sentence.

I questioned him several times in regard to the relations then existing between France and the United States, relations imperiled by our Mexican expedition. His answer was unfailing: "We have had enough

---

[1] Mr. Lincoln compared his position to that of a small boy in Springfield who had invested his savings in a pet coon. The animal turned out to be exceptionally vicious, scratched and tore his young master's clothes to rags. A passer-by, struck by the boy's disconsolate appearance, inquired what was wrong. "Hush, don't speak so loud, can't you see he's gnawing his rope off now? That way, I can go home and tell the folks I could not prevent his escape."

war. I know what the American people want and, thank God, I count for something in the country. Rest assured that during my second term there will be no more fighting."

Undated

The suddenness of my departure for Richmond with the Presidential party prevented mention of a meeting with General Butler and also of an interesting trip to Georgetown undertaken in company with a fervent Catholic convert, a Jewess of great intelligence and enthusiasm. We were shown through the Convent of the Visitation and that of the Georgetown Jesuits. The sisters of the Visitation have, for the most part, Protestant scholars and only a few Catholics. It seems that, among the former, conversions are frequent. The establishment is well organized but not equal to those I saw in New York.

The Jesuit school is fairly well kept, neither very good nor yet very bad. They too have both Protestants and Catholics among their pupils but here, the superior told us, almost all keep to their own religion and rarely change their faith.

I believe that the Catholic clergy in this country differ little from those of Europe; their members remain very conservative and are naturally sympathetic toward the South. There are two reasons for this attitude. The South has always shown itself more favorable toward the Faith than have the Puritan portions of the country. The higher ranks of the Catholic clergy are more in harmony with the aristocratic and royalist tendencies of the slave-holders than with the North. The fact of their having favored the South is a bad point for the Church, now that the triumph of liberal and democratic ideas has become an accomplished fact.

There is, however, a recrudescence of Catholic faith among New England converts. Though small in number, the group is important on account of the high quality of its exponents. This bleak rockbound coast, with its granite hills and boulders, has the faculty of initiating ideas and breeding strong men, so essential in monastic life. Such blood infuses a new spirit into the Catholic Church of America. But, as I have said, the number of conversions is small and I hardly believe that this movement will become popular. It is, nevertheless, highly interesting to observe its progress. I think that the only two denominations which are increasing at the present moment are the Presbyterian and the Catholic, the former making giant strides.

Though there is much talk about the spread of what they call Indifferentism, this to my mind is greatly exaggerated by its agnostic partisans. It hardly constitutes a real danger. As to Presbyterianism, it is generally speaking the religion of ardent abolitionists and is completely in accord with Northern Republican sentiment. It is the sect of Lyman Beecher and has received new impetus through the energy and indomitable will of its chief apostle. Beecher himself is largely responsible for the spread of his severe doctrine, which both in theory and practice is extremely austere. Thus, Presbyterian maids and matrons neither dance nor attend the theatre. I am acquainted with several families here who adhere closely to these rules. It is a notable application of moral theory to practical life.

I see from statistics that the intermediate sects remain about stationary or are even in regression. Everything that has to do with the aristocratic hierarchy which came from England remains static or is on the decline. This is the case with Episcopalians. There is a strong movement which causes America to reject everything contrary to the idea of equality among men or anything that recalls social caste. But, as there are still many who crave stability, so as not to find themselves see-sawed between one belief and another, these have taken refuge in the ancient faith and given it firmer footing in certain places. This does not mean that conversions are numerous, but it is certain that they exist. The Irish immigration and the constant influx of Germans who are Catholics make up the number. As for Indifferentism, I repeat, I do not think that this tendency is growing. Of course, there are many who care for no religion whatever; there always have been and always will be a great number of free-thinkers here, but no more now than in the past.

I told you that I had recently made acquaintance with the celebrated Butler, who professes the religion of success and has made much profit in its pursuit. From a Democrat he became a radical Republican, from a lawyer he turned into a general and was then sent as Governor to Louisiana, which at that moment was in ebullition. He tamed the feverish spirits and became the popular idol throughout the State. At the moment of danger, he was appointed Governor of New York City where his presence was worth an army. They knew that he would never yield ground, possessing, as he does, a sort of innate power which is remarkable. Unfortunately, he had the foolish idea of seeking military glory and met a terrible defeat at Wilmington. This did not abate his prestige nor reduce the strength of his iron hand. It is on this personage that the opposing parties now concentrate their powers of admiration or of hatred. . . .

During these feverish days I have by no means forgotten my duty toward God. Of course, last Sunday, being on the Presidential yacht, I was unable to attend mass. As to abstinence, I am obliged to live like a pagan. But what would you have? It does not prevent my being united with you during this holy week nor from embracing you with all the force of my mind and heart. Dear soul, I have constantly thought of you during this sacred season. Not that I do not carry you in my mind at all times. But what a spiritual blessing to be able to call up hour by hour your feelings, acts and gestures; in so doing, I feel myself beside you. Why repeat that you are never distant? Perhaps only because of my certainty that it gives you as much pleasure to read it as it does me to write it. Let us both pray for the future of this magnificent country, which you have your own reasons for loving.

April 12th

Washington has been in a state of frenzy since the taking of Richmond: shouts, speeches, fireworks, nothing else is to be seen or heard. The 10th of April was proclaimed a legal holiday, a day of thanksgiving throughout the nation. Exactly four years have passed since the first insurgent shots were fired and nothing is now left of the ambitious edifice of rebellion. The South is subjugated, trampled down. Its male population has been practically annihilated. Ruin, devastation and death—such are the results of audacious and absurd pretensions. I should like to invite our French Southern sympathizers to make the excursion from which I have just returned, study slavery on the spot, and become acquainted with the frightful details of this institution. In seeing the irons worn by these unfortunates, and the corruption of the society which, to an extent inconceivable to us, profited by their labor, they might alter their opinion of the regime. While we were visiting the wounded at City Point, one of them, whose leg had been amputated, asked us to look into the garments he had picked up when Petersburg was taken; they contained an instrument used to chain up the slaves on market days, an iron manacle confining the wrists so tightly that even a lady cannot put it on without great pain. What a way to civilize the African race! If ever the words of de Maistre, "The earth cries out and asks for blood" were true, it was surely in this country.

Just now, on all lips, the noble maxim, "forgive and forget" is to be heard. Columns of Confederate prisoners constantly traverse Washington. Not a hostile shout greets their passage. The population seems to avoid looking at them, as though not wishing to hurt the feelings of these misled creatures. At the same time, almost every citizen boasts of possessing the right formula for re-edifying the Union. He also realizes that virulent political discussions can lead to nothing constructive.

Richmond is now fed and supplied entirely by the "Yankees" and everywhere the words peace, pardon and clemency can be heard. It is impossibe to imagine the rapidity with which the temper of the North has altered and to what extent it is spreading everywhere I go.

Yesterday the whole town rushed out to greet General Grant, the moment his arrival was announced. According to the prevailing fashion, shouts of "speech," "speech," rent the air. The General had the good taste to sidestep a triumphal entry and the besieging crowd, failing to discover his hiding-place, was forced to give up the show. For my own part, I confess to having been much disappointed. I had looked forward to seeing what the reception would be like. But I can hardly blame the General for having chosen otherwise.

On Tuesday, a tall colored man knocked at my door, bringing a bunch of flowers and a note. Both came from Mrs. Lincoln. She told me that her husband was to address the crowd the next evening from the White House window and asked me whether I would like to listen with her to his speech, from one of the adjacent ones. Naturally, I accepted gratefully and found myself at the Executive Mansion before and after Mr. Lincoln had finished his speech.

It was a great event and a remarkable discourse, in which the President underlined his political conceptions and offered to moderate between the opposing parties. This solution does not seem to please a large majority; but the coming days will show what can be made of this idea. The ceremony concluded, Mrs. Lincoln took me through the White House. When we came opposite the President's door, she threw it open without knocking. There was Mr. Lincoln, stretched at full length, resting on a large sofa from his oratorical efforts.

When the President saw us enter, he rose impulsively, came forward and took my hand, which he held in his own a long time as though better to show his pleasure and affection at seeing me again. We exchanged several words on the subject of his address and the extremely moderate ideas which he had expressed therein. He spoke at length of the many struggles he foresaw in the future and declared his firm resolution to stand for clemency against all opposition.

I did not stay too long, in order to let him rest, and escorted Mrs. Lincoln down to the parlor where she habitually receives. A third person, Miss Harris, daughter of one of the New York Senators, completed our intimate trio. We talked at great length and on all sorts of subjects. Mrs. Lincoln, full of the triumphs of the last few days, spoke with quiet confidence of the future and showed great satisfaction and pride in her husband's success. But I must break off in order to catch the mail.

April 16th–18th

The clouds had gathered menacingly by the time Wednesday came. The President's address called forth violent reactions. On Thursday, a veritable campaign against him was launched. I had seen the storm brewing but do not remember whether I told you so in my last letter. However, in reading over my notes, I see that already on Friday I was trying to imagine what might be the results of his proposed policies, though never remotely suspecting what the future held in store only a few hours later. I came home, at about half-past five, from the post-office, after mailing my letter to you, and stepped into the church a moment, where I always sense your presence better. On emerging, I fell in with Mr. Sumner. He was returning from the War Office, where a long Cabinet council had taken place and where the President had given orders to keep the Confederate leaders, on their way to make submission to the Union, at some distance from Richmond. Before announcing this decision, he spoke with utmost firmness to all the secretaries present, for the most part hostile to his views, insisting upon the necessity of an attitude of clemency and pardon on the part of the victors. . . . I entered my lodgings after this conversation and decided that nothing should make me leave my rooms that evening.[1]

Suddenly, at about eleven, just as I was beginning to undress, one of the officers who is a fellow-lodger knocked at my door, calling out in a loud voice: "The President has been assassinated." I rushed out with him into the street, where the others joined us. We had not far to go—three blocks from where I live (about the distance from the Rue Chauvau-Lagarde to the Boulevard Malesherbes). Opposite the theatre where the crime had just been committed, a cordon of troops had been drawn up in front of the small house to which the President had been carried. The soldiers were crying like children but were also dangerously exasperated. Utterly impossible to get through the line or even to approach it. At the smallest move among the bystanders, they would have fired

---

[1] A marginal note to this letter, in my mother's handwriting, explains how my father had received an invitation to attend, with the Lincolns, the performance of *Our American Cousin* at Ford's Theatre that night, but that he had with some hesitation excused himself, not liking, even at the risk of offending White House etiquette, to attend a theatrical performance on Good Friday.

without hesitation. I remained standing thus for many minutes; no one had any news but all refused to believe that what was being repeated could be true or that such a horrible end as this was within the bounds of possibility.

All of a sudden I recognized on the doorstep that same Miss Harris with whom I had conversed at the White House such a short time before. The unhappy girl was spattered with blood but found words to tell me that the President was dead. A moment later, General Halleck confirmed her words, which however had not been quite exact. Slight pulsation could, it seemed, be detected, showing that the heart still beat. Sumner at the bedside clasped the President's hand, while Mrs. Lincoln, leaning over the small cot, vainly repeated, "Speak, speak." Her husband, who could not hear, remained motionless. This seemingly endless tragic scene continued throughout the whole night. At exactly twenty minutes past seven the heart definitely stopped beating. I will spare you any further details of this terrible drama. The newspaper accounts are perfectly true and will be reproduced in France, where you can read them.[1]

---

[1] Later, my father added to his account of Lincoln's life and death the following information which he had from Judge Otto, who remained throughout his life one of his most intimate American friends:

"The first floor of the house where the President had been carried consisted of three rooms opening on the same corridor. It was in the

At the very moment of this attack, another assassin had entered Mr. Seward's house and penetrated into his bedroom, where the Minister lay suffering from the serious carriage accident in which his shoulder-blade and jaw had been fractured. Young Frederick Seward was about to enter his father's door when the assailant fell upon this unexpected victim and left him for dead in the corridor. The assassin then rushed in, with the intention of dispatching the father. Perhaps his violent attack on the youth had exhausted the would-be murderer's strength. In any case, he could do no more than gash the Secretary's already wounded

---

small front room that the dying man lay. The bed had been moved under a flaring gas jet, which lit up the livid pallor of his face. Those nearest could just hear the faint sound of his breathing, which at intervals became quite inaudible. The surgeons held out no hope that he might, even for a moment, regain consciousness.

"Judge William T. Otto, who for thirty years had been intimate with Mr. Lincoln, clasped his hand. Mr. Speed, the Attorney General, and the Reverend Mr. Gurney, pastor of the church usually attended by the Lincoln family, stood on either side. Against the wall leaned Mr. Stanton, gazing fixedly on the dying man's face, seemingly over-whelmed with sorrow. From time to time summoned from the room, he wrote telegrams or issued instructions for the preservation of order in case of emergency.

"The rest of the Cabinet, together with several Senators and Generals, paced up and down the corridor; thus the long night passed. Toward seven o'clock the surgeon announced that death was at hand. At twenty minutes past seven the pulse ceased to beat. All those who were present seemed to emerge as from a trance as Mr. Stanton, approaching the bed, leaned over and closed the President's eyes, drew the sheet over his face and, in a low voice, uttered the words: 'He is a man for the ages.'"

face with his long knife and escape, his identity undiscovered.

At first, the news of this attempt on Seward's life aroused stupefaction and horror rather than violent anger and the desire to see justice done on the aggressor. It seemed as if the crowd had lost the faculty of reacting violently to such attacks. But, suddenly, there was a change that was equally unforeseen. The city came alive; the spirit of vengeance awoke and spread like flame. Cries, shouts, passionate exhortations rent the air. All over the Union the same was true, as soon as the telegraph wires transmitted the information that rebel leaders were responsible for the acts of that terrible night.

Woe to them! As I fear, the hour of reason struck at the same time as Lincoln's passing. Before that moment hatred and political strife were cooling. Now, passions are again furiously alight. Nothing we have witnessed in Europe can give an idea of what today can be seen and heard in the United States.

Washington patriots have draped their houses in black and wear crêpe bands on their sleeves; shops are close-shuttered. Lincoln's death, for those who loved him—his family, his kindred—for America and for me personally, is a loss forever irreparable. But for himself, I cannot feel that this is true. Tacitus, when addressing Agricola, said in his eulogy: "Never

98

wert thou so happy in the midst of life's triumph as now in the luster death has shed upon thee."

Nothing could better apply to President Lincoln, dying as he did at the very moment when the task so painfully accomplished had been achieved, when success, unhoped for in extent, had crowned these years of struggle. He leaves to his country both victory and peace at the very moment when almost insurmountable difficulties would have been his lot, when the halo of achievement, bit by bit, would have been torn from his brow, when, after having bestowed liberty on four million human beings and while promising clemency and forgiveness to all his adversaries, he was struck down.

I have seen many attempts to portray Mr. Lincoln on canvas and many photographs too, but neither painting nor camera reproduces, or is ever likely to reproduce, the expression of his face, still less will either suggest his true psychology. His arms, unusually long and powerful; his complexion, sun-burnt like that of a man whose youth had been spent in the open air, exposed to all the inclemencies of weather and the hardships of manual labor. His supple and vigorous gestures denoted great physical strength, also extraordinary resistance to privation and fatigue. Although the contours of his face were rugged, yet the broad high forehead, over great brown eyes deep-set under heavy brows, was unusually lined. His nose was straight and strongly marked. His lips full and yet delicately modeled. With the furrows which ran crossways from cheek to chin, the face appeared equally strange and strong, revealing remarkable intelligence, great power of penetration, tenacity of will and high-mindedness.

After passing some time with Mr. Lincoln you were left with a profound impression of poignant sadness. He was, however, extremely humorous, with a trace of irony always to be found in his wit. His stories bring the point out clearly. He willingly laughed either at what was being said or at what he himself was saying. Then, suddenly, he would retire into himself and close his eyes, while his face expressed a melancholy as indescribable as it was deep. After a few moments, as though by an effort of the will, he would shake off this mysterious weight and his generous and open disposition again reasserted itself. I have counted, in one evening, more than twenty of such alternations of mood. No one who heard him express personal ideas, as though thinking aloud, upon some great topic or incidental question, could fail to admire his accuracy of judgment and rectitude of mind. I have heard him give opinions on statesmen and argue political problems with astounding precision. I have heard him describe a beautiful woman and discuss the particular aspects of her appearance, differentiating what is lovely from what might be open to criticism, with the sagacity of an artist. In discussing literature, his judgment showed a delicacy and sureness of taste which would do credit to a celebrated critic. Having formed his mind through the process of lonely meditation during his rough and humble life, he had been impressed by the two books which the Western pioneer always keeps in his log-cabin, the Bible and Shakespeare. From the Sacred Writings he absorbed the religious color in which he clothed his thoughts. From Shakespeare he learned to study the passions of humanity. I am inclined to think that this sort of intellectual culture, since it aids in preserving originality, is better suited to the development of a gifted mind than is regular education. Originality explains Mr. Lincoln's talent as an orator. His incisive speech finds its way to the heart; nay, reaches the very soul of his listeners. His short, clear sentences captivate and his remarks become proverbs. It is he who, more than any other, defined the character of the war in these well-known words: "A house divided against itself cannot stand; this government cannot continue to exist half-slave and half-free."

True, he was never one of those rare and terrible geniuses who, once possessed of an idea, curb and sacrifice others to their imperious will; but, better

101

than any, he knew the exact will of the American people. Amid the confusion of discordant voices, which are always heard in moments of crisis, he distinguished with marvelous acuteness the true voice of public opinion. He had nothing in common with the politicians who follow popular caprice. His firm will, exalted nature and, above all, his inflexible honesty, kept him ever aloof from schemers. Feeling that he was the people's agent, duty compelled him to stand by his principles. He was well aware that in a free democracy close union must always exist between the authority which represents the nation and the nation itself. The tendencies of his mind were all liberal. Slavery seemed to him unquestionably unjust and, for that reason, hateful. He had found in the Declaration of Independence the principle of liberty and equality. Long before he became President he firmly stated, in a celebrated controversy with Douglas, his adherence to these principles.

Such a nature was admirably constituted to direct an heroic struggle on the part of a people proud enough to prefer a guide to a leader, a man commissioned to execute the popular will but, as in his case, strong enough to enforce his own.

Lincoln is now the greatest of all Americans. The tragic prestige which assassination lends its victims has conferred upon him a superiority over Washington himself. When I told him the other day, while passing Mount Vernon, that its name and that of Springfield would some day be equally dear to American hearts, I little thought it would so soon be true or that now Springfield would perhaps even surpass the other in their affection.

As soon as Mr. Lincoln had expired, General Halleck with Sumner in the carriage went to the hotel where Johnson, Vice-President of the Republic, lodges. Mr. Sumner did not get out, so the General alone announced to Johnson that he was now President. The interview was short and frigid; the announcer said only: "With a view to your personal security, I advise you never to go out except in a carriage and accompanied by a sufficient guard." This did not take more than three minutes: Andrew Johnson had become the nation's chief.[1]

I hardly thought that authority could be passed so easily from one who was great and popular into the hands of a man who has yet neither power nor personal prestige. But such is the law! No one imagines that there will be any reaction against Johnson's decisions. He has become head of the nation without the slightest contest.

---

[1] At ten o'clock he took the oath of office, administered by Chief Justice Chase in the presence of a portion of the Cabinet and several congressmen assembled in his room at the hotel.

The first question to ask is: What sort of man is he? I have seen him twice, first on March 4th when in a state of inebriety he delivered a senseless speech; the next time, at City Point the other day, when he encountered the Presidential party. Hardly a sign of greeting then passed between them and, naturally, I was not introduced. However, we must never judge too much by appearances. He is a man who has a heaven-sent gift of intelligence and energy. As a tailor, at twenty, he did not know how to read, but at forty-five he made several speeches which were really admirable. He is a Tennesseean, carried away by ambition. He has become what over here is called a politician, which in Europe corresponds practically to a demagogue. The American politician is almost the reverse of a statesman. He was then a Democrat and a partisan of slavery but changed his opinion in 1859 and delivered his best speeches against secession, an idea which had become popular at that time. A year later, he was elected Senator and, when Tennessee seceded from the Union, he remained faithful to the Federal flag and gave up his seat in the Senate. At the beginning of the war, he was sent as military governor of his State and acted with indomitable energy at a time of extraordinary difficulties.

In changing his opinions, or rather his flag, he

became a radical and it was because of his varied talents that he was chosen as Vice-President. In recent years, a victim of family tragedies, he has sought consolation in alcoholic stimulants. But, strong-willed as he is, after the lesson of March fourth, they say that he has mastered himself and not for a single moment has shown weakness in this regard. Yesterday he was in perfect moral condition. Such a man must naturally have scores of enemies. His first words were that henceforth he would have none. His next were to declare that he would retain all his predecessor's Cabinet ministers, at least for the time being. But this will not prevent the great change which is surely coming.

Lincoln was for mercy at any cost. Johnson is partisan of those who favor the banishment or even the death penalty for the guiltiest among the rebels. His proposed solution for the reconstruction problem in the South is most radical. At this moment, the Southern States have only the rights of territories; they must prepare new constitutions and the Federal Congress will examine and pronounce whether these constitutions are in accord with the laws of the Union. It will also decide whether they are to have the right to re-admission as part of the United States.

Meanwhile, the rebellion has taken away all their former rights and privileges. This doctrine will be applied with an iron hand. I fear also that on the

Mexican question he intends to adopt a very unfavorable attitude toward France. His origin and his antecedents are entirely Democratic. Hence he belongs to the wrong school. When I think that France's agents have always favored this party, how can I refrain from a contemptuous shrug of the shoulders? Though I have serious reasons to fear his influence and his decisions, I try to tell myself that I must not too hastily jump to conclusions and that responsibility and new power will perhaps moderate his actions.

Vengeance on the rebel leaders is the universal cry heard from one end of the country to the other. Lincoln's recommendations are forgotten. Yesterday, anyone might have thought that a million men had not been sacrificed, so strong was the sentiment inciting to pardon. Today, all idea of pardon is obliterated; certain Southern politicians have asked safe-conduct papers to enter the Northern zone. Mr. Lincoln had signed two of these Friday evening; they have been revoked and orders given to arrest the two men. Yesterday, a rebel general, prisoner of war, was brought through Washington. He was almost lynched by the crowd and only escaped by virtue of the protection of armed forces. From what I see I am led to fear that blood will flow in this city. The town is politically divided. Among the citizens there are a great number of Southern sympathizers, who are called Copperheads (the smallest and most venomous of serpents). There are, of course, a still greater number of ardent Unionists. A clash between these elements is possible, I might almost say, probable. If so, do not worry unduly, for I promise that, in case of fighting, I shall go to the Prussian Legation, the most popular of all, and remain with the Minister in his own house. As to the possibility of trouble, it is far from being negligible. Associations have been formed against the Copperheads. Yesterday a man told me quite offhandedly that he had just joined one of these societies.

The recent discoveries of the plots and intrigues which preceded the assassination might cause an outbreak. It is known that the whole of Good Friday was passed by the conspirators in assuring the murderer's entry into the President's box. The door had been loosened on its hinges. They had filed the locks and placed tiny chips of wood in the bolts to prevent any shutting of the door from the inside. Every difficulty had been foreseen and any chance of failure guarded against.

The director of the theatre, a well-known "Copperhead," left for Richmond that very evening. All of which indicates that the assassin was not without accomplices. Among the letters addressed to the President from many different points in the Union, one especially, from New York, has been found in which the writer says: "Yesterday, when sitting in a restaurant, I heard some men at the next table speaking about a plan to assassinate you, together with Seward, Johnson, Stanton and Sumner. This was scheduled to take place a few days hence."

It is certain that Johnson escaped today almost by a miracle. In his hotel, they have discovered, in the apartment directly above his room, an arsenal of pistols and knives. The man who owned them arrived on Friday and immediately asked to speak to Johnson. By good luck, the Vice-President was not in, so that after the attack on Lincoln the visitor escaped, leaving his weapons behind him.

I do not feel very comfortable about poor Sumner. But I must say that he is intrepid. On the way to Richmond, he said that there might well be a bullet waiting for him, but that he was prepared for it. I thought the idea was chimerical then. Today, it seems more than probable. In this country, it is certainly difficult to know what precautions can be taken. It would be impracticable for an American to go and live at one of the foreign legations. Meanwhile, threats of death are heard everywhere. The Government is taking energetic measures against leaders in the South. It seems that Johnson, with the personal courage which so often characterizes the American, takes a sort of pleasure in defying the dangers which surround him.

April 21st

Since my last letter, events have taken shape much as they were foreseen. Johnson's presidency seems to be approved and accepted by the entire nation. He is in full possession of his faculties, will and presence of mind. Everyone agrees that his drunkenness was accidental. It seems that, on the morning of March fourth, he was given an overdose of opium before leaving for the Capitol and, during the lamentable scene which followed, was suffering torture. However this may be, he is now behaving circumspectly.

Is he, from a political standpoint, equally sage? I have difficulty in believing it. He is always saying: "I'll show them; I'll teach them that treason is a crime, the greatest of all crimes, and that it must be punished." Certainly we must admit that President Lincoln was the only man in America strong enough to voice public opinion and yet be able to affirm that there is a power above Justice, which is Mercy. His successor is incapable of employing language of this kind; but he might at least take another attitude and, if only out of respect for his great predecessor, remain silent. Unfortunately, he does everything in his

power to envenom this terrible side of the question—
how chastise treason?

Here, precisely, is the difficulty involved. Where
does treason begin and where cease? What is its first
degree and what are its extenuating circumstances?
Who must be hanged? The governors of each rebel
state? Or the military commanders? The ministers
belonging to Jefferson Davis' cabinet? Or Jefferson
Davis himself? I took the liberty of advising one of
the President's friends to recommend him to study the
history of the year 1816 in France and ask himself
whether Marshal Ney and his confederates, steeped in
treason like Jefferson Davis, should have been judged
guilty.[1] Has France any reason to congratulate herself on Ney's execution? This is what I want to suggest for Mr. Johnson's meditation, but I fear even such
a pointed lesson will hardly give pause to his violent
tendencies.

---

[1] Michel Ney, Duke of Elchingen, Prince of La Moskowa (1769-1815),
one of Napoleon's most famous marshals. After the Emperor's abdication, he offered his services to Louis XVIII but when his old leader
disembarked from Elba and marched triumphantly on Paris, he could
not resist joining Napoleon's forces, thus contributing to the success
of the famous hundred-day campaign. Arrested after Waterloo and
indicted for high treason, Ney was summoned before a military
tribunal. The court martial refused to sit in judgment. He was,
however, condemned by the House of Peers and shot the following
morning. His popularity remained undiminished and is attested by
the heroic-sized statues which decorate the principal square of Metz
and the Luxembourg Garden in Paris, scene of his execution.

Meanwhile the Government is hunting down the democratic newspapers. In all the small towns, crowds besiege the hostile press because they were adjudged by curbstone trial as accomplices of treachery. After having burned the buildings and thrown the presses into the gutter, the mob disperses, satisfied. It is no sinecure to be a journalist belonging to the opposition in this country these days! In Paris, the job is more profitable. The Government first sends warning to the offender. When this is known, the journalist has a public ovation and no measures are taken against him. Here, when a newspaper office is sacked, it hardly yields material for "an item," as they call it.

All this demonstrates the truth of my favorite axiom: Liberty is a force which, in governmental hands, is greater than any despotic power.

I am trying to discover in Johnson a governing thought but have as yet not succeeded. To punish traitors may be the order of the day, but afterwards what? He is a radical to be sure, no one denies that, but what sort of radical is he?

Just now a reorganization of his Cabinet is being talked about; if he modifies it, we may expect ferocity rather than moderation. Stanton, who is War-Minister and who enjoys the reputation of being the most radical of radicals, would become Secretary of State in Seward's place, and Butler—the Butler of New

Orleans, who ruled there with an iron hand and is universally feared—will become Minister of War. This choice, if it be maintained, will reveal the true spirit of the administration.

I have seen Butler twice recently. He seemed like an old acquaintance. He is well known and well liked in France. After Prince Napoleon's *coup d'état,* he sat in the Council and in the Senate of the Empire. He was created Minister, Prince and so forth. In 1848, placed at the very pinnacle, he began by storming the city halls and became Prefect after the second of December. Here he poses as a liberal. Up to a certain point, he has renounced all thought of making a *coup d'état* for himself. Even he could hardly dream of such a thing in this country, but, short of this, he will encourage every kind of violence. Add that he is extremely able, and you have the explanation of how people feel about him.

I firmly believe that it is impossible to compute as yet the loss this country has suffered. Without any doubt, Mr. Lincoln was embarked on a course which was perilous even for himself, but he alone could have followed it. Without him, there is no way out. Only the common road, where nothing can oppose the radical program.

The President's assassination was far from being an isolated act. This is now almost certain. There were many accomplices. The other designated victims all had narrow escapes; it is an abominable story. Will Europe and France at last understand what ferocious passions were engendered by slavery?

Yesterday was the day chosen for Mr. Lincoln's funeral. The ceremony was divided into three parts: inside the White House, the procession from there to the Capitol, the ceremony under the great dome. At the executive mansion, the number that entered was necessarily small: State functionaries, delegations from Illinois and Indiana, also official representatives from three other States. I went in, side by side with one of the ministers, and, as all the servants at the White House know me well, was given a good place. The East Room had been arranged for the ceremony. The catafalque (in the center) was draped in black with impeccable taste; the coffin covered with silver was more doubtful. Stands had been erected around the room. There, we were all so tightly packed as not to be able to stir hand or foot; and there we remained two hours by the clock. The chief mourners were the Speakers of both houses, Lieutenant-General Grant, and Admiral Farragut, head of the Navy. I waited for Grant's entrance with much curiosity, as I had not yet met him. Suddenly someone said: "There he is!" In fact, he had just taken his seat. He is a small man, with a face impossible to analyze. He wears his auburn hair short and badly cut. Like the greater number of army officers he has a full beard, which is also reddish. His features are irregular, his expression very gentle. One suspects that he still bears the traces of former excesses. Indeed, in his youth, he was considered a drunkard. His wife succeeded in curing him, reduced him to sobriety and thence helped him to fame. But marks of former dissipation still remain in his countenance. What seems the most striking trait in Grant is great reserve. He lets nothing be noticeable in his dress, which is most simple, nor in his bearing, which is extremely modest and which does not for a moment suggest military triumph. In looking at him, anyone filled with our European ideas would find it hard to realize that this same man, a fortnight ago, annihilated an army eighty-thousand strong.

The service began punctually at noon. In the midst of religious silence four clergymen belonging to different denominations prayed in turn. The President had been quite a fervent Presbyterian, so that the first place was given to a clergyman of that confession. We had to submit to an hour's discourse by Dr. Gurley. He has the sort of eloquence belonging to this denomination; that is, no high-sounding phrases but a stock of dry commonplaces marshaled in good order. At half-past two o'clock, the procession began to move. Two thousand yards separate the White House from the Capitol.

They had to be covered. The guests assembled in the East Room found seats reserved for them in the carriages. At the head of the procession was the new President, surrounded by a triple escort. There was reason to fear that he might be a victim to the same fatality which had struck down his predecessor. Behind us, on foot, came delegations from every imaginable society and from every State. In the middle, a mass of Negroes followed their liberator. Under burning heat and a blanket of dust, marching at a snail's pace, it seemed impossible ever to reach the Capitol. Once arrived, bathed in perspiration, I, for one, declared to my carriage companions that I would not risk my lungs in an ice-box where pneumonia lay in wait for its victims. Many evidently felt the same way and did not remain for the last rites. I left my card for poor Mrs. Lincoln. She had not recovered her mind since Saturday morning and is still completely insane.

Today I had a long talk with the Colonel in charge of police investigations. He has proof indicating that there are some fifty individuals implicated in the plot. He seems quite sure too that the principal assassin is still in Washington and, according to custom in America, an immense reward is offered for his capture. Remember that over five hundred thousand francs are promised to the man who takes him and there seems little doubt of his arrest. I inquired if the

Colonel believed that the rebel leaders were involved in the plot. Such was not his opinion.

As for the interior situation, there is no possibility of having any clear notion of what the future may hold in store. Anything can be expected, now that the great Peacemaker is with us no more.

Dear soul, I must finish this letter in haste, without even rereading it. It is four o'clock. Only time to hurry to the post-office before the mails close.

April 23rd

You inquire into my material situation and what I spend on these faraway shores. Here is my simple budget. From Amiens, where we parted, till my arrival in New York, I spent one thousand one hundred and fifty francs. The steamer ticket alone amounted to seven hundred and fifty. On board, it is impossible to live economically. There are all sorts of extras, and a person obliged to change money is apt to lose a good deal in manipulating unfamiliar currency. A more serious detriment is neither to speak nor yet understand a single word of the language spoken. That was my case from Amiens to London, and from London to Liverpool.

The first days, I ought to say the first months, were very expensive. It is inevitable that the stranger should be exploited. My first period in Washington has, on the contrary, been quite moderate—about five hundred francs a month.

What is terribly dear in America is clothing. Aside from this item, you can be quite comfortable at a reasonable cost. This last month I have been practically independent of hotels. I rented a room in town and arranged to take meals at a boarding-house. This is much cheaper, but you can readily understand it would never have been possible had I not learned some English. Without that, I could have done nothing useful: merely sleep in a hotel and follow the crowd. On the subject of language, I may say that it is going pretty well. Everyone I meet is full of praise, and refuses to believe that I have been at it for only three months. I succeed in conversing without trouble and even entertain my interlocutor. I have more difficulty when it comes to understanding what is being said around me. I have to do a good deal of guessing and confess that I often guess wrong! When this happens, I am obliged to step warily in order to avoid saying something silly.

Politicians are more and more inclined to hang people. This has become for them an absolute need. Someone told me yesterday that the telegraph has recently transmitted a hundred thousand messages containing the verb "to hang."

I make every effort to tell those I see that this is pure insanity. All my rhetoric is employed in preaching moderation, but when I think I have converted one, another escapes me. It is an ungrateful task, and very wearing. When driven into a corner by argument, they only repeat: "It has to be. It is the will of the people." What answer can you find to that? I tremble at the thought that they may take Jefferson Davis. There might be a chance for the others, but in his case . . . As for exile, they threaten to apply this punishment very widely.

I believe I wrote, two or three days after Mr. Lincoln's death, that the thirst for revenge would be ferocious. I had no conception then that it could possibly go so far; at present, it is utterly disgusting to observe. Clergymen from their pulpits, newspapers, associations, public meetings and the people at large think and speak of little else but vengeance.

Ask your father to dictate a note on the Mexican question in its relation to Rome. It would be most important that I should receive this as early as possible. Does the Pope sustain Maximilian? Here—and I repeat again—I have not a single French newspaper. The only articles I read are from the London *Times*.

April 28th

The telegraph has just brought news of M. Rouher's[1] speech on *Mexico and the United States.* It seemed, on reading it, that it might have been taken from my own despatches. He employs the same reasoning and the same method of composition. If so, I have not been much mistaken in my deductions. Since the capture of Richmond, and other events in the South, what a series of new arguments might be added!

At last, that horrible Booth has been caught. He was hunted like a wild beast. They learned that he was in Virginia. A considerable force was sent after him. The farm house where he was hiding was surrounded, and then began a drama unlike anything which could be seen in Europe.

Booth was with an accomplice; they were known to be armed. The usual demand for surrender was made. And it seems that a violent altercation between the wretches was audible. Booth shouted to Herold, his companion, who proposed to give himself up, that

---

[1] Eugène Rouher, 1814-1884—a statesman of extraordinary eloquence, many times Cabinet Minister, and elected president of the Senate, was often characterized as "Vice-Emperor." His most important interventions in Parliament were his speech on Mexican affairs and, later, on Italian unity. Like Guizot, he was an implacable enemy of Thiers.

he was nothing but a coward, and persuaded him to resist further. At this, the soldiers applied torches to the farm building, so that the flames should force the inmates to a parley. A few moments later, the heat becoming unbearable, Herold opened the door and, holding his arms aloft, made the sign of surrender. The soldiers tied his arms, but Booth, encircled by flames, remained motionless, pistol in hand. Hereupon, one of the soldiers opened fire and stretched him out, almost dead, on the barn floor. The bullet had lodged in nearly the same place as the one he had fired at Lincoln. He still breathed when they carried him out. On being asked whether he had anything to say, he replied: "Tell Mother that I die for my country." An instant later he expired.[1]

---

[1] In the year 1881, in a letter to Nahum Capen, Edwin Booth, for the first time, consented to speak of the tragedy:

"I can give you little information regarding my brother John. I seldom saw him since his early boyhood in Baltimore. He was a rattlepated fellow, filled with quixotic notions. On the farm in Maryland he would charge on horseback through the woods 'spouting' heroic speeches, lance in hand. . . . We regarded him as a good-hearted, harmless though wild-brained boy, and used to laugh at his patriotic froth when Secession was discussed. That he was insane on that point no one who knew him well could doubt. When I told him that I had voted for Lincoln's re-election, he expressed deep regret and declared his belief that Lincoln would be made King of America and this, I believe, drove him beyond the limits of reason. I asked him once why he did not join the Confederate Army, to which he replied: 'I promised Mother I would keep out of the quarrel. I am sorry now.' Knowing my sentiments, he avoided me, rarely visiting my house except to see his mother, when political topics were not

The President's assassination brought about unimaginable reprisals. Yesterday I saw an officer just returned from Sherman's headquarters. When the news first came, there were four hundred prisoners in the camp. No human force could have prevented the soldiers from falling upon them. After a few minutes, not one remained alive. To make things more complicated, it now seems certain, alas, that some of the highest-ranking Confederates in Canada instigated the plot and that the blow was directed by many of the Canadian agents high in the Confederacy. If so, instead of being or seeming to be an act of single political vengeance, it is one of wide complicity and nothing can prevent large numbers from being condemned and sent to the scaffold.

Foreign affairs are not going too badly. This morning I had a long discussion with Johnson about Mexico. After M. Rouher's speech, I declared frankly that it would look badly on their part not to keep quiet. I have been told that Johnson has by no means given up the Monroe Doctrine and its great destiny,

touched upon. He was of a gentle, loving disposition, very boyish and full of fun, his mother's darling; his deed and death crushed her spirit. He possessed rare dramatic talent and would have made a brilliant mark in the theatrical world. All his theatrical friends speak of him as a poor crazy boy, and as such his family think of him."— *Edwin Booth*—Edwina Booth Grossman—*Life of her father.* Century Company. 1902.

but that he was keeping this relic of a Democratic past up his sleeve. My informant added, however: "If he keeps it in his Bible, certainly he does not read all of it at one time and has not yet got to the essential passage." Four or five of his friends have succeeded in getting around him and are preaching moderation. Thus we may expect that a good deal of time may pass during which France will be able to bring home her glorious flag and leave Maximilian free to do all he wants. Thus we can declare, with M. Rouher, that we are entirely out of it.

The Northern Army is disbanded. The order and regularity I was sure would be theirs appear everywhere. Each volunteer regiment is assembled, entrained and sent back to the place where it was mustered. Upon arrival, the soldiers are thanked and sent back to their pre-war occupations. All this is accomplished with extraordinary ease. As to those who have lost one or more limbs, they are assured of a good pension and that ends the matter. The idea of supporting an unoccupied loiterer is alien to the American mentality. Besides, at this moment, America still retains under arms from two to three thousand men. The regular contingents of other days (fifty thousand) will be increased. There is also an independent force called the Hancock Corps, recruited under the name of this popular chief, and colored regiments totaling one hundred and twenty thousand. A certain number of volunteer regiments will be reorganized. These units are supposed to police the South, inculcate respect and love for their conquerors among the brave rebels, sweep out all the banditti that infest the country, and calm down the political passions still burning hotly.

The danger to the public peace comes from the disbanded soldiers roaming the South. This I have written about before; what can be done with men whose occupation is gone, whose farms are destroyed and who have lost not only their livestock but the indispensable farm workers who were their slaves? These unfortunates have neither hearth nor home, and while the Federals who are, after all, good people, are still feeding the people down there, this cannot go on forever. What will become of the Southerners who have not either the habit or knowledge of work?

Unlike the Northerners, there are few artisans among them and you must know that this population —however gentle and charming they may appear and, as Escandre proclaims, still are—undoubtedly possesses certain fantastic traits together with the constant practice of handling gun or revolver. I would advise those who expect to govern the South to suppress the weapons of those who plan to go to Mexico, lest they might decide to overthrow Maximilian and treat him as game.

I forgot to tell you that I have adopted the customs of the country. I breakfast at 7.30, lunch copiously, and dine at five in the evening; when in Rome you must do as the Romans do. I have hardly time enough to say how I love you, though I say it over daily to myself. Your letters are so sweet, tender and kind that I thank you equally tenderly for them. Have I any need to say that my life, soul and thoughts are yours? That I never conceived our union could be so intimate and profound as to enable me to feel happy here so far off? To feel this as I feel it, I must now believe what before seemed impossible.

May 5th

Pacification continues with prodigious rapidity. Not a day passes that the papers do not contain news of the surrender of the last rebel contingents. Fifteen days hence, there will hardly remain a single man under arms from the Potomac to the Rio Grande. This horrible war, which has seen two million men *hors de combat* and cost both Federal and Confederate America between seventeen and eighteen billions, which has destroyed the political life and the social fabric of the South, has nevertheless liberated four million slaves and transformed America into a first-class power. But that is already ancient history, *the war is over*, there can be no guerrilla warfare here. All the population would rise up to put it down. South Carolina, so lately the storm center and soul of the rebellion, has other things to think about and accomplish than to play politics. She is in a condition of utter starvation. She defied the enemy and the enemy's hand has come down and crushed her under a terrible weight.

I have here, under my eye, the text of three discussions which took place in our French Legislative Assembly. M. Thiers'[1] speech on liberty seemed to me very feeble and narrow-minded. He believes that real liberty is to be found in the parliamentary regime. I cannot think that this is so. In America, which has not a parliamentary regime, you do have government for the people and by the people, a different thing. I was much disappointed and disillusioned to find the most illustrious representative of liberty in France speak-

---

[1] Louis Adolphe Thiers, 1797-1877, lawyer, journalist and historian of the French Revolution, Consulate and Empire, renowned for his uncompromising opposition to the Second Empire, during which he was imprisoned and sent into exile. The apparent relaxation in the severity of the regime encouraged Thiers to return to Paris. He was elected deputy in 1865 and consistently exposed the fatal blunders of Napoleon III. His statesmanlike qualities and enthusiastic patriotism made him the acknowledged leader during the Franco-Prussian war, after which he was elected President of France.

ing so poorly and in such a rococo manner. Besides this, now that I read English, I find more and more that our French tongue is terribly weak. What a difference from the political language of America, where such staggering blows can be dealt verbally; where the speaker and writer possess an enormous vocabulary of strong, vigorous, energetic words which enable the orator to go straight to the point, without phrase or periphrase, and to smash his adversary with the force of his attack. This language, in its plainness and strength, is singularly adapted to political combat. I was all receptivity on beginning Thiers' speech, but found myself rudely awakened when I plumbed its emptiness.

In the debate on Mexico, M. Rouher says substantially what I do. But he exaggerates and parodies my thought; by over-affirmation he makes me overshoot the mark in discussing America. Yesterday—and only yesterday—I at length received the debate about Italy. It would be too long to tell you what I think of M. Thiers in this connection. Certain things he says are quite beautiful and charming, but there are also, according to my view, statements that are quite false. Take, for example, what he says about American churches. The principle here is that when a hundred persons of the same faith desire to found a church, they associate themselves and form a legal corporation, buy a lot, build their church and designate a pastor or ask for a parish priest and, with him at their head, the religious unit is set up. If there were twenty million Catholics, the procedure would be the same. These are the methods here. No state intervention, no public functionary, no established church. But the force of these separate churches constitutes a pillar of American society, to be employed as society thinks fit.

Do not imagine that I propose to import this organization into France, but at least I may be permitted to believe that my conscience would be just as free without any temporal power to back it. Suppose that the Pope should leave Rome, would that greatly trouble the Catholics in America? I claim that they would not even notice it. What Thiers says of Venice and of Florence is descriptively fine—the democratic city of Veronese and of Titian, the aristocratic town of the Medici and of Michelangelo—these two centers of beauty have little resemblance to each other; but do you think perhaps that New York is like Boston or that either resembles Richmond? He speaks of the "sectionalism" of towns—the word is American—but, in America, it is rather the sectionalism of the State. New England, an example of its type, is unique. Perhaps it has some traits in common with Piedmont, but I can assure him that it has not a single point in common with Tennessee or with Kentucky. Nevertheless few would maintain the theory that the United States is not today one people and a very great one.

Thiers' speech suggests many other remarks. But I would rather talk to you about something different. In my opinion, M. Rouher, though too violent and too personal, is from beginning to end nearer the truth.

Pardon this tirade, my dear soul, it is in answer to your observations on the famous speech, and I know you like to have my impressions. Discussions which take place in the French Chamber or, in fact, French affairs in general, fail to attract the slightest attention over here; none but Mexican questions can obtain a hearing and, even so, only short news cuttings or brief quotations are mentioned. There is a great feeling of admiration for the *name* of Napoleon, though nobody for a moment thinks of imitating Napoleon's ideas of government. This sentiment is vague and purely theoretical.

The nation, as a whole, favors the New Italy and admires Garibaldi extravagantly, which does not mean that they know anything whatever about his policies. Just as I have said of their cult for Napoleon, their ideas concerning him are nebulous. They do not like the English but that does not prevent Americans here from being proud of their English descent or

128

from taking an immense interest in the affairs of Great Britain. The most popular nation here is Russia. Why? Impossible to say. There seems to be no reason —just a matter of taste, like any other. A curious case comes to me as an example. The sentiment was so strong in favor of Russia that the Russian Minister was able quite insolently to take the part of the South without calling forth the slightest criticism from any American. The most susceptible persons just say: "Poor old Stockel, he used to play cards with Benjamin Riddle and his set. He can't help missing them. That's only natural." No one dreams of bringing up any reproach against him. All this is perfectly true and without exaggeration; it shows that Europe, her affairs and her sentiments, count for absolutely nothing. America is a world outside—a people entirely different. The Mexican question is cause of some slight bitterness. This manifests itself when the Emperor is spoken of. They are impatient, but do not want to quarrel with him. He is, after all, a Bonaparte! All the same, they satisfy their grievance by speaking of him with a flippancy which is thoroughly American. The *Herald* makes fun of his book, which they dub a complete failure, and warn him that when he is obliged to quit the throne he need not hope for a place in their office as military critic, because his book is too poor. Criticism stops there.

After all, what characterizes America is that the citizen is himself. He has his own institutions, his own beliefs. He is not a European but a thorough American. There is a development constantly taking place which may or may not be measured by an outsider. But no one who really knows them can say: here are people who bear a striking resemblance to Frenchmen, Germans or Russians—no, they do not in the least resemble any people but themselves.

England has, to represent her in Washington, the best diplomat she possesses, Sir Frederick Bruce. His program is evident. He intends to accumulate on France's head all the indignation which this country has piled up against England during the war. To succeed, he must prove himself a very strong man and a good negotiator.

May 12th

Last night I dined with the Prussian Minister; he had invited Sumner and myself alone, but on arriving we found two other guests in the parlor. One we already knew, the other was very modestly dressed in gray and was no other than Governor Aiken of South Carolina. This white-haired old man, clothed almost poorly, was, four years ago, proprietor of an immense domain and owned more than a thousand slaves. Victim of the recent terrible reprisals, he was seized by order of the Government, a week ago, brought by force to Washington and has been placed on parole out of respect for his former high position. The Prussian Minister, thinking that it might be helpful, invited Mr. Sumner to meet him. It turned out to be like mixing fire and water, an encounter between the angel of wrath and the fallen angel. To commence with, greetings were of glacial politeness. Sumner began by asking news of some former Southern colleagues in the Senate, only to receive the invariable response: "He is dead, he is in hiding, he has nothing left." It was like a bad dream. After that, the broken old man told his own tragic story in lighter vein, as though it were almost a joke. For months and months hardly five minutes passed without a bomb falling on Charleston. The town was almost deserted, but theft had become an industry and the robbers risked no matter what number of bullets in order to pillage the dwellings; often both thieves and their loot were laid low at the moment of getting away with it.

In his own case, Sherman's soldiers did not come to steal but to destroy. He possessed a magnificent service of English silver for which, before the war, he had paid seven thousand pounds. The soldiers did not take the trouble to carry it off, but merely threw it onto an immense fire they had built to roast a pig.

Among the sufferings and privations of all sorts he had gone through was the fact that his wife became insane. At this point, the atmosphere grew chilly and there were long silences during which the two adversaries closely observed each other. The one had suddenly become almost timid, in spite of his efforts to remain stoical; the other was embarrassed to find himself so triumphant before this human ruin.

After dinner, Sumner, visibly moved, took me aside and exclaimed: "But this man is a traitor, he was involved in the affairs of the blockade-runners, his case is terribly bad," and as though afraid of allowing himself to show pity for this instigator of civil war, now victim of his own machinations, he finally fled precipitately from the house.

Never have I seen such a melancholy contrast. As our talk proceeded along the same lines, the same answer inevitably followed when any name was brought up. "He's a prisoner now. He was with Johnson in Tennessee. He is dead. He was with Lee . . ." If there is anything worse than civil war, it must be the days that come after the war is over.

To descend from the general to the particular, I spoke with Governor Aiken about the Lasteyries, whom he knows exceedingly well. I asked what had become of their plantation, he replied: "Naturally, no more slaves, but the ground is still under cultivation. The Federal Government has, I believe, established a colony of freedmen." I asked whether the property could still be considered valuable; he answered: "Very much so." It therefore seems urgent for Ferdinand de Lasteyrie to put in his claim; should his property be handed over to him, he could surely make something out of it. Tell him about this and about Governor Aiken who seems to be a real friend of his.

May 16th

I can't possibly tell you what pleasure the sight of your dear image and that of darling Thérèse gave me. What a delight to see you! It allowed me to pass the whole morning gaily, as though stimulated by a breath of fresh air.

You inquire into what sort of life I live here. I thought I had furnished you with all the details. I am in a house which is a complete facsimile of those inhabited by hundreds of Americans of the middle class, where several families dwell under the same roof, eat at the same table, and pass their evenings together in the same parlor. It is a sort of Phalanstere, a social communism whereby even some quite rich Americans avoid keeping house. As a matter of fact, it is difficult to find servants; the choice between

Negroes and Irish is hard to make; although the Negroes make better servants, I cannot say that they are quite perfect. In the first place, the colored man is apt to take all he finds. In the second, he is lazy. In the third, as to his morals, they are something awful. That is, perhaps, why so many Americans prefer to live as in a family pension, or boarding-house. I have many reasons for doing the same. It is cheaper; I hear and speak exclusively English; finally, it is more cheerful. You cannot imagine how agreeable and polite everyone is. There are four or five married couples, never a breath of altercation between them. Not a quarrel outside. Each goes about his own business and that of his children. Toward me, all of them show thoughtful kindness. I have a large room, two windows with a fairly good exposure. During the last month and a half, we have been literally stifled. The table is very good and the small privation of doing without wine is no longer such for me. Nevertheless, I should have left before this, had not Mexican affairs kept me chained in Washington. I cannot leave yet, for another reason. The case of Jefferson Davis, and his trial, may modify my plans, for there may be something that I can do for him should his neck be in danger, and this is a signal service I would certainly try to render.

May 19th

My dear soul, all these days my mind has been absorbed by the trial of Mr. Lincoln's assassins and also of Payne, Mr. Seward's assailant. The debates are extraordinarily lengthy and, as it is customary to allow the cross-examination of witnesses by the defense, it makes the work of one who, like myself, is obliged to follow the dialogue closely, quite complicated. Yesterday I attended the session of the military commission, which got together all the actors and reconstructed the scene. Admission is very difficult and I had to get tickets. Faverney[1] of our Legation, and his wife, also wished very much to be present and, as I knew all the participants, I took them with me. Mme. Faverney was so much interested that I felt obliged to remain there the whole day myself.

Imagine an oblong hall; at one end a barrier, extending from one side to the other, separates the spectators by a few yards from the bench of the accused. Mrs. Surratt is first in line. She seems completely subdued but, from time to time, darts a glance

---

[1] Comte de Moreau-Faverney, second secretary of the French Legation. Became first secretary in 1869. From 1865 to 1866 the French Minister was the Marquis de Montholan. He was replaced in 1867 by M. Berthemy.

of hatred toward the judges. A few feet off, a soldier is placed in order to prevent communication between her and the one next to her. Each of the prisoners is in irons, hands and feet chained, so that there is a great show of strength and all precautions are taken to prevent these horrible wretches from killing their judges. In the center of the hall two large tables are installed, covered with green baize. The military commission is seated at one; reporters and stenographers at the other. The lawyers are grouped between the Commissioners' table and the barrier which separates them from the accused.

As I have told you, great liberty is permitted the lawyers for the defense. They interrogate the witnesses quite as they please. But I noticed that certain questions brought forth unexpected answers which were disastrous to their clients, so that they themselves abandoned a system which reacted against them. One of these wretches, the perfect type of villain, is Payne, assailant of the Sewards, father and son. He was recognized by the four house servants as being the man who inquired for the Secretary, penetrated into his bedroom and dealt the blow. At sight, it is impossible not to believe in his guilt. The others are all ignoble-looking or else possess faces utterly devoid of character.

The case against these criminals is only of interest

136

for me when the subject of politics is treated, and when Jefferson Davis, or the government at Richmond, or the Confederate agents in Canada are brought into question. Thus, a witness who had served in the rebel army was asked:

"Did you ever hear any talk about the assassination of Mr. Lincoln?" He responded:

"Yes, indeed, they talked of little else in the Confederate Army, where funds to pay the assassins were raised."

Another was asked what had been said at Richmond. The answer came immediately:

"An association had been formed there to pay the assassins; the Government was to contribute what was lacking."

Surratt was in Richmond April 8th, and on his return he brought back gold. He said that he had talked with Jefferson Davis and Benjamin, then Secretary of State. He left for Canada and returned again April 13th; you know what happened on the 14th. At length, they brought out a document which was apparently overwhelming evidence against Davis. It was a letter signed by a man who had submitted a plan for the destruction of Northern towns and on the back of this abominable paper Davis had written, in his hand and over his signature, these lines:

"As to the plan for burning the vessels and towns,

etc., the preparations are in the hands of Professor MacColough. They are known only to him and to one other person.

"President Davis asks for an interview with General Harris, formerly member of Congress from Missouri; he also desires the Secretary of State to be so obliging as to interview General Harris and find out what means there are for overcoming the difficulties encountered up to now in the application of the plan."

This document, dated February 20th, is signed J.D. and was received on February 17, 1865.

I saw several witnesses acquainted with Davis who declare they recognize the penmanship of this autograph discovered in the archives of the Secretary of State.

The Generals belonging to the military commission requested me to look at the autograph, at today's session. They say further proofs will be submitted against Davis. I know that one of the lawyers for the defense has said: "If I were a judge and my decision was based on the procedure up to now I should condemn Davis for the assassination of President Lincoln."

This brings me back to Jefferson Davis and his ultimate trial; so far no decision has been taken as to the time or place, but the question is of extreme gravity. President Johnson is quite decided to have him tried; on what accusation, I wonder. As a murderer, or as a traitor? That is the point in debate. One of the most influential people here went yesterday to see Johnson. The President told him that it was impossible to foresee the consequences of such a trial. As you will readily understand, many political questions will be brought up shortly and nothing could be more interesting for me than to attend these discussions. So I have decided to remain here indefinitely.

I can't describe the pleasure your dear letters give me; they do me a world of good. I assure you that I am in excellent health, moral and physical, and mentally active as I have not been for a long time. I take the best care of myself, my meals are regular and moderate and here, where almost every one drinks to excess, I remain as sober as a desert camel. Those who believe that America is in danger are mistaken from A to Z; she has only internal difficulties to cope with at present, embarrassments, if you like, but, as to perils, those are all in the past. There is nothing to say but this. Our French Copperheads will have to swallow the triumph of the North and reconcile themselves to the fact that the future is assured and more than assured.

May 21st and 22nd

I am beginning to write today, Sunday, because I foresee that tomorrow I shall be completely absorbed by the case of the seven wretches who have been taking up so much of my time during the past week. They are indeed vile specimens, unmitigatedly so; not a redeeming feature; just low and vile and nothing else. But the case becomes interesting because of what the examination brings to light concerning their accomplices. Every endeavor is made to show that the original plan to assassinate the President was intended to be carried out on the Fourth of March, on the inaugural platform itself, where Booth was standing close to Mr. Lincoln. If he did not kill the President then, it was because means of escape had not been prepared nor yet enough money collected for his flight. The next day the conspirators are said to have met at Mrs. Surratt's, quite in despair and believing that the project had been abandoned. She revived their hopes and despatched her son to Richmond.[1] He returned on the 3rd of April, saying that he had seen Davis and Benjamin and had carried letters to the

---

[1] As the trial proceeded, my father's belief in Mary Ann Surratt's culpability was shaken. She was, however, sentenced to death with the other conspirators.

plotters in Canada. One of these, Thompson, their ex-Minister of the Interior, opened an account for him at the Ontario Bank. Booth and his associates were thus supplied and the murder was committed. More, they allege that letters from Benjamin have been discovered asking that the crime be accomplished without delay because of the deplorable state of the Confederacy. Meanwhile, they represent Davis as arranging to have the Northern cities burned and preparing to introduce yellow-fever germs into New York.

That is the story of what was going on in Richmond. It passes for true evidence, and this is what Europe dares to take seriously. I need hardly tell you that the trial of Davis is now sure to take place. This man, no matter how superior he may be, is nevertheless very guilty; no one yet knows whether he will be tried here or in Richmond. I must also tell you that Johnson's intentions are moderate. He will not allow any but the assassins of the President to be executed; the rest will have mercy shown them and, in the future, there will be no more military tribunals.

All would go finely were it not that this awful Mexico may, at any moment, reappear in an acute and unexpected way. This is how the case stands: Texas, which has recently been detached from Mexico and incorporated into the United States, remains rebellious. Worse, the Governor, Zebel, and the General-in-Chief declare officially that they intend to resist and that they count on the help of a foreign power. Moreover, Maximilian, in his constitutional decree, omitted to mention that there was any frontier between Texas and himself and simply defined the limits of his empire on the north and northwest, on the south and southwest, and not on the west. This forgetfulness constitutes a stumbling-block; taken in conjunction with the Rebel declaration, it indicates secret collusion between them. Here, there was not a second's hesitation in deciding that the United States must hasten to take the Texan territory out of these Mexican hands. Yesterday Sheridan, who is an incomparable cavalry general, left Washington to assume command of a hundred thousand men and march immediately into Texas.

On the other hand, President Johnson certainly wishes to maintain peace with France. I suggested to him: first, to send a general to the Texan frontier, on a diplomatic mission, so as to prevent Sheridan from committing any infraction of international law; secondly, to come to a frank understanding with the French Cabinet in Paris and make it clear, after comparing dates with acts, that if by any misfortune Maximilian has been mixed up in this recent rebellion, there is no power on earth which could prevent the

United States from exercising her right to suppress these bands of Mexicans.

Johnson, I must repeat, sincerely desires peace. He would be ready to sacrifice much in order to avoid complications of this sort; he knows about as much as did Mr. Lincoln himself about foreign political questions, which is to say, nothing at all—literally nothing. He leapt eagerly at my suggestions. If it should turn out to have been useful to bring about a declaration of this kind, to which France can so easily respond, it may be said that I have done a real service. I recall a personal anecdote concerning poor Mr. Lincoln which indicates his historical knowledge. When I compared the capitulation obtained by Grant and Sherman to the unprecedented triumph of Napoleon at Ulm in 1805, I saw that he did not understand what I was talking about. So, I explained to him in what the success of Austerlitz consisted but was left in doubt as to whether he had ever heard of this battle.

I saw a man from North Carolina the other day and inquired whether he had on him any Confederate paper. He drew from his pocket a bill for five dollars (25 francs). I procured it for you to give François. The building represented on the lithograph is the Capitol at Richmond, the portrait that of Jefferson Davis—consequently, worth absolutely nothing!

Yesterday evening, I made a call on a general of my

143

acquaintance and found there an officer who walked back with me. It was raining hard, so we took shelter under a shop front just as two soldiers passed by. One of them was roaring drunk but continued to stagger along, while the other, planting himself before us, addressed us in quite incomprehensible English. As we remained silent and motionless, he cried out to his comrade in indescribable but unmistakable French: "Are you afraid of these fellows, that you run away?" —"No, I am not a bit scared," retorted the other, coming back, while I laughed and began to speak to them in French, which was in fact their native tongue. They turned out to be old soldiers, one an ex-zouave, the other a simple infantryman. Both had come to settle in America, where the ex-zouave developed strong anti-slavery opinions and willingly engaged to uphold them. He had come back that very day with Sheridan's cavalry. The other, on the contrary, had strong Confederate sympathies and had been picked up by their conscription as an American citizen. As the rain still poured, I stood and enjoyed their dissertation on the American Army as compared with the French. The ex-zouave, who was the less drunk of the two, explained his ideas, which were not so foolish after all. Addressing the American officer, he began to lecture him: "Captain, I don't want to offend you, but it is right that you should know that our French

Army is the best in the world, no mistake about that, France being the first of all nations."

"What is he saying?" exclaimed the officer.

"Nothing, just that he is drunk," I replied as the soldier went on:

"In spite of the respect I owe you as my superior, permit me to explain in Latin, since you do not seem to understand French:

" '*Errare humanum est*.' Learn from me that to have a good army you must have two things: discipline and patriotism. Just look at the rebels. There were patriots for you. I love them almost as I do the French but that didn't prevent me from giving them some good knocks. I don't say that the Yankee isn't brave too, but he does not understand a thing, not a single thing, about fighting and, as for discipline, he does not know the first word about that. Perhaps, we French might teach all of you something, if we put our minds to it. They aren't really so stupid, these Yankees, but they do need education. Yes, Captain, with all due respect, education is the sinew of war."

How I laughed at the spectacle! The Captain, happily, understood nothing of the soldier's discourse. Had he done so . . . As for me, I never saw my fellow-countrymen behave so completely in character.

What I have been fearing has happened. I am asked to take charge of a batch of high-ranking French officers, on their way up from Mexico, who are particularly recommended to my attention. They want to attend some of the trials. All are literally bowled over by what they have seen of the strength, activity and wealth of this country. On the other hand, they are far from being impressed in the same way by Mexico. You should hear them describe conditions over there. And yet they have the cheek to think that I could get their claims recognized by America. It is almost an insult to my intelligence to propose such a thing seriously. I encouraged them to talk and I assure you that what they told me about the Emperor and the Empire was most edifying.

May 25th

The news that M. Drouyn de Lhuys is interested in my work here may perhaps bring about what I desire more than anything else just now, that is, to be charged with the claims of our French citizens, no matter what my official title. A regular appointment is necessary; without it, I should soon use up my credit with the Government. After the third claim, they would send me packing and my sources of influence would soon be dried up. It is poor policy to cut down a tree to get the fruit. In the first place, my knowledge of the ground is now worth a good deal. I am beginning to know the ropes thoroughly. I am sure that if they thought they were doing the French Government a favor by treating me well as regards these claims, they would do so at once. As for asking me to take care of them, as an individual, I could hardly do so. Indeed, I could not do so at all, effectively, for it would be impossible to succeed with more than two cases; after that, they would consider that they had taken trouble enough to please me personally and would pay no attention to further requests. After a while, without an official position, I could not have adequate reason for remaining longer in Washington. I have not written to Paris, and shall write nothing to M. Drouyn de Lhuys on this subject, but shall leave that to your father, in whose hands I place myself and my interests. Yet I must say that here, incontestably, is a great opportunity, if they are disposed to make me benefit by these circumstances. Our French Legation has proved itself incapable of following these questions intelligently or giving useful advice, so that the choice is open and depends only upon Paris. In regard to pecuniary questions, there are two ways of dealing with them: either to leave me as now, with the same salary, and allow me to arrange about fees with my clients—there are regular tariffs for this kind of work and they are very high; otherwise I could be given a fixed salary. I am ready to accept their decisions on this point, though I prefer the first solution. If I succeed in making good and defend my countrymen's interests satisfactorily, I believe that will be the best way of meriting the gratitude of the foreign office.

You will understand from my recent letters that the Mexican question is now hanging by a single thread. These affairs must be looked into closely; they cannot be settled in a day but need time and close care. I confess that if you were by my side I should not have the slightest aversion to remaining here permanently. We could live in tranquility and begin to put some hay into our boots. I repeat, that in order to write about this country, one must go slowly. Effective study requires an atmosphere of serenity. It requires much time and reflection. If your father could arrange this with the Minister of Foreign Affairs, nothing in the whole world could be better. I should then ask you to join me here as soon as possible.

I must know that I stand on firm ground, make no mistake from the start, and play the game with caution. I feel confident that my work is suited to my kind of intelligence. My qualities—even my defects— should be a help and not a hindrance.

You can testify that, these four months past, I have not taken the slightest action to advance my career, afraid that by doing so I might interfere with your father's plans. The path is so plain and familiar that I feel I can succeed in it better than in any other. Moreover, should I not, there would always be time to revoke my official title. Whatever happens, be certain, my dear soul, that we shall not be separated much longer. Either you will come to me or I shall go to you; so courage, fortitude and confidence! I am with you, heart and soul. I can say no more than that. Meanwhile I embrace you accordingly.

May 30th

I have just finished a twelve-page report to Drouyn de Lhuys, in which I detail the procedure of what they call here "the criminal trial." I have translated and analyzed the whole scrap-bag. It would have been impossible to have given myself a harder or better English lesson than in following the technical details of this litigation, together with all its terms of daily life. In the end, I have come to certain conclusions which may, perhaps, seem in contradiction to what I have told you previously. I will set them down, as they may interest your father.

Firstly: It seems certain now that where there was constant talk in Richmond and in the Confederate Army about assassinating the President.

Secondly: Davis was informed of some of these

projects—and himself questioned his war minister about them.

Thirdly: Surratt, one of the assassins, was in Richmond on April 1st. He says he saw Davis and brought him gold, without saying whence it came.

Fourth: The trial brings to light the horrible details of the treatment inflicted on Federal prisoners but there has been no material proof brought forward that Davis was cognizant of the assassination project.

Consequently, it must be admitted that Minister of War Stanton and Judge Holt were often mistaken or, at least, went much too far. Stanton will soon pay for his errors by a considerable diminution of prestige and power. The question of Davis' treachery remains to be decided. Whoever has borne arms against the United States is punishable with death. That is the text of the Constitution, reaffirmed by two laws, one of which is dated 1862. It applies to the rebels. That Davis is doomed is, if not certain, very probable. However, they are making no haste to try him. Nothing has been decided, either as to the place or the time. Any delay is in his favor. Possibly between now and then the violence of opinion may wear out and result in a return toward clemency. During these last few days there seems to be a tendency in this direction.

As to the other prisoners, Stephens, Fletcher, Campbell, Hunter, etc., they run no great risk. Though nothing is yet settled, I believe that their cases will simply be dismissed.

The proclamation of amnesty is soon to appear. But it must be admitted that it is extremely rigorous. The categories are very lengthy and the loss of civil rights so generally applicable that, in certain States, the number of those excluded from them is larger than that of those allowed to retain them. This state of things is transitory but, while deploring it, I recognize that it may be necessary until final reorganization. Now that the war is completely over and that Mexico, for a time at least, will remain dormant, these are the questions to be studied in order to comprehend what is going on. . . . Touching the claims, should I, by singular good fortune, obtain title to their settlement, our financial situation would be assured. But, I repeat, I still ride the hobby of hoping for an official title which would give me increased influence.

At present, Johnson and others constantly ask small services of me. With an official status, these would become important. But don't worry your head over all this. Rest assured that I am ready for whatever befalls me and will not let myself get depressed should fate be contrary; neither will my head be turned if it prove favorable. Before any question of my return comes up seriously, you may know that my heart beats hard at its very mention. During these last days I have made extraordinary progress in English, understand almost everything that is said and talk without making too many mistakes. I amuse myself reading Milton, whom I extravagantly admire. What force and what poetic grandeur!

Dear soul, you are the object of my most ardent, anxious and profound emotion. The human tongue, either in French or English, is inadequate to express all I feel. I can only say how near I am in thought and, in the depths of my heart, entirely with you as I was five years ago. This letter will reach you almost on the anniversary of our marriage, darling girl. What thanks I owe you for the happiness you have given me and all the affection the future holds in store. Be strong and courageous. I can say no more without breaking down. Adieu, adieu.

June 2nd

How will you be when this letter reaches you? These days of waiting, as I need hardly tell you, seem interminable; but I know your courage and have perfect confidence in the future which lies before us.

Tell the dear little one that I will love him well and that he will always have a place in my heart beside Thérèse and beside his mother. I have passed these three days in hard study and have prepared a despatch that is particularly delicate and difficult, on the amnesty and reconstruction proclamation. It is composed of systematic analyses which are extremely complicated to draw up. I am satisfied in advance that no one will attempt to get ahead of me in explaining them! As far as work is concerned, this is my curriculum. I am quite absorbed in my reports, in which I have dealt with the most difficult points in order, and that means a great deal of concentration. There are even some considerations, relating to the future status of the liberated slaves, that I have been at for fifteen days and which I shall hardly be able to send before another fortnight. When I finish with reconstruction and slavery I shall make a few visits, read Milton, or do nothing particular until I return to work again. In recapitulating my past small doings, I can tell you that what I have handled best is the Mexican affair, which I understood clearly from the start. When everyone was shouting "the United States is going to invade Mexico with 100,000 men," I was alone in declaring that not a man of them would budge. It has now become evident that no one will ever budge unless unexpected complications develop. The great danger has passed, as I foresaw and wrote. I must add that I did everything in my power to persuade the Government to remain quiet and circumspect. It took a lot of haranguing but, frankly, I think they really agreed with me before they were ready to admit it.

As to the Davis affair, although France refuses to be concerned as to whether he is doomed or not, I believe that it will be good policy for her to preach the doctrine of clemency. If she would only consent to take real trouble in this, perhaps . . . perhaps . . . But, up to now, little has been expected of her and the trial has brought out atrocious details. Lee, the chivalric, did nothing to prevent the Federal prisoners from dying of hunger in Charleston; Beauregard is said to have stationed them under Federal fire. Lee thought this quite normal in warfare and Davis gave orders accordingly. It is not strange that the North shows some ill-will to them now.[1]

I begin to think, dear girl, that it will be on this continent that we shall find ourselves reunited. Since this morning I have been working over an endless despatch. I shall write to my family by the next steamer.

---

[1] The writer of the above passage, whose information was drawn from highly partisan sources, was then unaware that the Southern army was long on half rations and that the failure of the resources of the Confederacy had reduced the population, rich and poor, to extreme want. President Jefferson Davis, in 1863, frankly stated to his congress that his government was sadly lacking in *men, meat and money.*

June 4th and 5th

I can't say that I am thinking of you particularly, for the thought of you never leaves me a second. My very soul trembles as I count the hours and the days . . . yet, nevertheless, I feel strong and work my best, though living here in a temperature which represents between 44 and 48 degrees centigrade; that is to say, we are smothering. I assure you, it does me no harm. I never yield to the temptation of drinking between meals when I take tea and coffee with rum. Thanks to this regime, I do not feel at all "low." Yesterday evening, there was a breath of air. At eleven, the Secretary of State called for me and we went for an agreeable drive until half after midnight. If there were not such grave questions to be dealt with, I should absent myself for a few days, but I do not yet see the possibility. I write very long reports on the movement of opinion in the terrible Davis affair, and believe that I am right and, at the same time, doing a good work in thus trying to prevent blood from being shed. Nothing is certain yet. It is hard to foresee what will happen. It seems that moderation is making headway, but the current moves slowly. Opinion tends to divide into two camps. The Republicans' assertion runs as follows: To hang Davis won't do any good; we have no guarantee against the South, who gave him up as a holocaust, hoping thereby to get themselves out of trouble with no other sacrifice demanded of them. What we want is Negro suffrage. The slave of yesterday must be armed against his master. He must be given the right to concern himself with his former master's doings. If he is kept down, as before, all we have done counts for nothing and the freed slave will be oppressed as formerly. The Democrats reply: Public opinion demands victories. Well and good, these you have had in plenty; profit by them, rest on your laurels, but leave the South alone!

Happily, the most powerful of the two parties contains elements which continue to preach clemency. You will realize that I try to turn all this into lengthy communications to our State Department, taking my subjects one at a time, never dealing with two different matters in the same despatch. I develop the arguments pro and con, describe the status of the case to date, and translate the significant extracts. Thanks to this system, I have now learned to put English into French, at sight, with perfect ease.

I enclose a letter which is certain to interest you. It comes from one of the highest placed public men in America, a radical Republican, probably a future

Senator, perhaps a future Secretary of State.[1] In it, as you will see, he speaks of Negro suffrage, also of the reorganization of the South; but the reason I send it is that knowing how much you like compliments about your husband, I believe this letter will satisfy your exigencies by showing that your aforesaid husband is not doing half badly over here.

Somehow today, dear soul, I have not the courage to talk politics, Negro suffrage, nor yet of Jefferson

---

[1] The eminent personage alluded to was the Prussian-born Carl Schurz, graduated from the University of Bonn (1848). He joined with Gottfried Kinkel, Professor of Rhetoric and founder of a subversive paper in the rising of '48 and '49. When the latter was condemned for twenty years in the fortress of Sandau, he was rescued, thanks to the skill and devotion of his comrade. Obliged to leave Germany, Schurz lived in Paris by his pen, in London by his teaching, until he could emigrate to the United States. During the political campaign of 1856, he made stump speeches in German. After naturalization, he practiced law in Milwaukee and soon became an influential member of the Republican Party. Schurz stood up stoutly for Lincoln against Douglas in the Convention and was appointed Minister to Spain when Lincoln was elected President. He resigned this post in order to enlist on the breaking out of the Civil War. Rising rapidly, he was commissioned Brigadier General of volunteers (1862). Two months later, he assumed command of a Division in the Corps of General Sigel, with which he took part in the second battle of Bull Run. Promoted Major-General in 1863, he commanded a Division of General Howard's Corps at Chancellorsville. At the head of the 11th Corps, he fought at Gettysburg and subsequently at Chattanooga. On the cessation of hostilities, he resumed his law practice and was chosen U.S. Senator from Missouri. He opposed some of the principal measures of General Grant, whose election he had ardently supported. Intimate with my father and Senator Sumner, he was at the latter's bedside on the eleventh of March, 1874, and pronounced his funeral eulogy.

Davis. I shall resume my usual habits next week. I want to talk, not about how I feel nor what I do, but only about how much I love you, dear girl, you and our little family, present and to come. Distance, uncertainty—I must not say anxiety—seem to bring us nearer. I keep counting incoming steamers. There are more now than before the war, and I have the satisfaction of counting on their better speed.

June 12th and 13th

I have literally worked all day and finished a long despatch. You can form no idea of the many things which constantly make trouble for me; those of today are the beginning of a series to which I attach great importance, having undertaken to clarify the thorny questions touching the reorganization of the Southern States. For this, during the past month, I have been accumulating documents; I cut out, paste and make copies of newspaper items, arrange digests of laws or debates and a whole lot of other things. Being, as I am, the only Frenchman in America capable of making sense out of these complicated problems, I must do what I can to justify my presence, while profiting by my advantage. Moreover, these questions alone constitute what might be termed "active politics," for

I do not lose sight of the advice you give me in this regard.

At present, Jefferson Davis awaits his fate at Fortress Monroe. Bets are even on what this fate will be. Nothing can be done about it, one way or another. As for Mexico, I have already told you that I remain the only one here to sustain French interests. They are now dormant—sleeping, I hope, the sleep of the just. Little or no interest is ever shown here in foreign politics. President Johnson has a sole idea in his head: Reconstruction of the South. I believe I possess all the possible information on the conditions under which readmission to the Union will be accorded the seven Rebel States, what passions they have set aflame, what social transformation they are causing. So there seems nothing better to do than to take up my pen and write, write, write on these questions. In so doing, I bear in mind that Fournier[1] explained servitude in Russia when no one but he could make it comprehensible because no one else attempting to do so had the slightest notion concerning that institution. I must also keep in mind that my subject is vast and beset with thorns and brambles. These must be cleared

---

[1] Ernest Fournier de Flaix, 1824-1898, a noted journalist who specialized in social questions and wrote authoritatively on the conditions of servitude in Russia.

away before I can explain all that is going on around me.

Now and then I come upon a fragment of some Parisian newspaper, translated and reproduced by the American press. Some are interesting, if only because of their stupidity and shortsightedness. Thus the *Patrie,* brought over in a recent mail, asserts that the Republican Party, "drunk with blood," is giving itself over to demagogic excess. I have rarely heard or read such a mass of absurdity compressed into so short a space. Those who are keen to shed the blood of Davis are *Democrats* not *Republicans;* and, frankly, I don't believe that either party, at this moment, is sanguinary. And yet a great President has been assassinated, the whole Government was doomed to share a like fate, and other atrocities were planned. These crimes are generally known. Why be astonished that there should be indignation about them? Surely, if vengeance were ever lawful or excusable it would be so in such instances as these. Nevertheless, I feel justified in the hope that no blood will be shed. Yes, we may really hope that this new people, which Europe likes to declare *barbarous,* is actually the most civilized in the whole world. You cannot imagine, though, what dangers menace the present Government. Since Saturday, new plots have been brought to light. The President is always guarded and his carriage escorted by twenty-five men. Conditions are serious. How can the North remain perfectly calm and serene?

The Papacy, according to my views, shows itself very wise in taking this new and realistic attitude toward United Italy. True, it strengthens the King's position immensely but, on the other hand, I do not believe that the country could have been left in a state of complete religious disorganization. It is understandable, though, that many must be raging over all this. What, for instance, will M. Thiers say now, after having solemnly asserted that anybody must be insane who conceives that there could ever be reconciliation between the Pope and United Italy?

Whatever anyone says, it is a triumph for the Emperor. I read in the English press a correspondence between the two "cousins." What a good lesson! I look vainly for a parallel in the history of any other royal family!

You tell me that Montalembert has written about Lincoln. I know someone in Washington who takes the *Correspondent* and shall look up the article. What an astonishing thing it is that in order to be understood by his countrymen such a man as Lincoln had to be assassinated! But these present demonstrations of posthumous admiration, like those we are witnessing, cannot be said to produce much effect here.

Sumner goes on repeating: "You Frenchmen always remind me of Cobden's saying to Guizot, 'Be strong yourself and then you can count on us to protect you.'"

Praise, after victory has been achieved, is hardly convincing; it always seems a bit forced. Nevertheless, the article may be of interest over here, should it have the luck to be translated for one of the important New York papers.

Your letters now come regularly; I have just received that of May 29th. We are approaching the moment about which I am burning to have news; something tells me that the event has already occurred,[1] I cannot explain why, except that my spirit suddenly felt light as if it could penetrate space, so near I felt to you. My love goes out to my little family. Kiss Thérèse and the newcomer; you may notice that this word can apply alike to the masculine or feminine gender.

June 18th and 19th

Today I went to Mount Vernon and yesterday visited the freedmen installed at the ex-residence of General Lee. This is how it came about: I had asked the Under-

---

[1] My mother wrote in the margin of this letter, "Pierre de Chambrun was born June 11, 1865."

Secretary of War to give me a pass in order to inspect the freedmen, being anxious to investigate the working of this new social experiment and to form an independent opinion about it. He invited me, instead, to go with him, the next day, to Mount Vernon, where he was taking his family on a private boat. I naturally accepted and even asked whether I might bring the Faverneys along. I like to show some attention to members of our French Legation. (The trip was accordingly arranged.)

So today, Sunday, we started at four o'clock on the poor *River Queen*, which had taken me to Richmond on that unforgettable occasion and which belonged, then, to Mr. Lincoln. At five, we touched at the Mount Vernon landing and climbed the slope where the residence is situated. It is now in the hands of a society of American ladies, who keep pious guard over the house without changing anything or touching the Washington souvenirs.

The building, a characteristic dwelling of a well-to-do British gentleman-farmer, is intact. I saw several resembling it as I went through England. There is nothing particularly distinctive about it. If you wanted to find subjects of contrast out of which to make fine phrases you could probably discover them, but not in the exterior of the house. You would have to go back to Washington's own time and evoke the transformation of the country between then and now, more particularly in Virginia, where nothing remains of the great social and political edifice Washington created and where he played such an outstanding and heroic part. Men like him, from overseas, cool, energetic, courageous—great gentlemen, after all—have totally disappeared from these regions. At least, since coming here I have not encountered any such type. . . .

Tell your mother that the name of George La Fayette[1] was pointed out to me, scribbled in his writing still visible on one of the walls. The famous key of the Bastille is in its place but is no longer a sensational novelty. There are now two or three prisons of the kind, not far off, where a man can be locked up, on short notice, just as easily as in the old Bastille destroyed in 1789.

Those who care for sunsets would have appreciated the superb afterglow we admired on our return. The river, the range of tree-crowned hills and, below, a whole forest of shipping would have made a splendid picture, but I will abstain from trying to give you even a verbal description.

The previous day, as I have said, we visited Arlington, the magnificent property of General Lee in Vir-

---

[1] During the terror, Lafayette's only son, who was named after Washington, was sent over to America and placed under his namesake's care at Mount Vernon.

ginia. It lies nearly opposite the city of Washington. The residence, now confiscated, is inhabited by Federal officers, while the agricultural domain is operated by a freedmen's camp, the organization of which is singular. It consists in a sort of village, composed of wooden houses built at some distance from one another, occupied by about eighteen hundred liberated slaves employed in cultivating the soil. These are given free food and lodging, for themselves and their families, besides wood for heating and cooking. Educational facilities are supplied for the children, while each farm laborer receives twenty cents daily, the working day being reckoned at twelve hours. The little colony enjoys the comforts consistent with simplicity. Living thus, in a state of liberty, just as in that of slavery, this prolific race continues to multiply. They seem satisfied; there are few quarrels. They eat, sleep and mill about without any subject of grave discussion among them.

I was much interested in seeing the magnificent dwelling of General Lee, charmingly situated on a height overlooking the Potomac. Alas! what has become of its former master? A homeless refugee, tracked down and hunted like a malefactor. There is an attempt to keep up the garden designed and laid out by his own hand but the officers in residence have boarded off the parterres and dug a row of graves for those who were killed in adjacent skirmishes. Strange anomaly, the house itself is filled with souvenirs of George Washington, for, as you may remember, Lee himself is a descendant of Washington's stepson, General Custis and in the old days the great George himself often slept under the roof, where the stars and stripes now majestically spread their protecting folds over the rebel mansion.

This week, Washington is writhing under a spell of torrid weather. As you know, I am not much affected by heat, but certain precautions must be taken: the principal one, to my thinking, being abstinence from liquids at meals or else absorption of hot tea only. This advice is not apt to be followed by those who eat ice cream and swallow cold drinks all day long.

I retain my room but lunch and dine at the club, which is better and not at all expensive and where they have a French chef. Certainly French cooking should, like our flag, spread over the world! When dining, one realizes the truth of this patriotic song and feels what a pleasure it is to be French! Nearly all the Washington bachelors come to the club for their meals and readily acknowledge French culinary superiority. It takes eighteen hundred years for a nation to learn cooking.

June 23rd

Today I have just finished a long report on what they call over here the "poor white trash." It has given me more trouble than any so far. I have been at it for over three weeks. Information is scarce and hard to get at; but I think I have managed to disentangle most of the snares. I consulted an acknowledged specialist, found him in perfect agreement as to my conclusions and, not until I had this assurance, did I set them down in permanent form. Do you realize that this made my twenty-sixth despatch, large-spaced like my letters to you and written on ministerial-size paper. They average from ten to twelve pages. Now I expect to treat the liberated-slave question, immigration, then Reconstruction and all that this will entail. America, at this moment, is completely absorbed in the ideas which appertain to these subjects.

The President has not been able to find a single hour during the past month which he could consecrate to foreign affairs; so you see they flatter themselves in France when they represent the United States as preparing to swallow Mexico. They are not thinking of Mexico at all.

I don't go so far as to pretend that the question is dead, but I can assure you that it is comatose. Of this

I am pretty proud, for when I began to handle it, truth was rather hard to discern amidst all the clap-trap talk which was far from clearing the air. But I was right in saying that there was no real danger, however difficult things might have looked. Just now any American you might ask would be sure to say: "We want to go to Mexico." If asked "When?" he would reply "right off." And if further inquiry was made "Why?", the answer would be: "To enforce the Monroe Doctrine." This dialogue has become universal. I have heard it myself a thousand times. For all that, you need not believe it is serious. Once having spoken out, no one thinks of moving.

At present there is nothing doing nor will there be until December. Then, when Congress meets, there will probably be several absurd motions. Should these come up when I am in Washington, I think I can promise to help get them buried in the special committees of both House and Senate. This will be easy because, at heart, those whose business it is to accomplish these feats agree with me perfectly and only get going when they are spurred on by the Press.

Therefore, if things can be stabilized in Mexico, we still have time. It remains to be seen whether tranquility can ever prevail in the Empire of Maximilian.

Regarding M. de Montalembert's[1] desire to come to America, you can assure him that he will be well received, but perhaps without much enthusiasm. He ought to know that his opinions concerning Italy are far from popular over here.

There are, of course, quite a number of American Catholics, but almost all of them are in the South and even these have no liberal tendencies. It is really essential that he should be prepared to know that America, as a whole, is steeped in Garibaldian sentiment and strongly for "United Italy." He will hear these ideas expressed everywhere and, loudest of all, throughout New England, where Catholics are looked upon as far from sympathetic objects, you might indeed say as worse almost than barbarians. To their minds, the Italian affair is considered as a victory over popery. As I have told you, when our friend Sumner wishes to show admiration for anyone he compares him to Garibaldi. Besides, the Pope is generally thought to have been partial to the Confederacy and, believe me, it is far from fashionable here to flaunt such sentiments. Except for these reservations, Montalembert may enjoy himself greatly in the United States.

---

[1] Charles Forbes, Count de Montalembert, 1810-1870, liberal statesman and author, renowned for his eloquence and for his defense of Catholic education. He was elected to the French Academy in 1852. He warmly espoused the cause of Poland and of Ireland.

June 27th

At last I have succeeded in finding Montalembert's article and have read the first part translated into English. I recognized brilliant marshaling of thought and phrase, such as clothe his best and most ardent inspiration. But it cannot be denied that there are many mistakes, some of them enormous. Thus, when he says that no newspapers were suppressed in America, he quite forgets or is ignorant of the real facts. For example, in 1862 the New York *Daily News* was put out of business by an order signed by my friend, Mr. Dana, Under-Secretary of War. The same year the *World* nearly shared a like fate. In many States, quantities of news-sheets have been suppressed outright, either by military order or by riots. Moreover, Congress has passed truly terrible laws authorizing confiscation. In the North, all property belonging to Southerners has been seized and, in many cases, sold. I, for instance, occupy a house owned by a Rebel. As a result, seizure, confiscation and sale followed. At the same time, individual liberty has suffered as much as in France. Prisons are full of unfortunates arrested two or three years ago and still awaiting trial. I can cite the case of a man from Tennessee

170

who has been confined in the Old Capitol prison since 1862.

When Montalembert declares that this war was *humane,* he must be dreaming! True, in certain places and circumstances, but what would he say of Sherman's march? The General commanding the Engineers Corps of this army told me only yesterday that a whole sixty-mile stretch in South Carolina, from Savannah to Goldsborough, has ceased to exist. Fire and sword have laid waste everything near the line of march. In looking back now, though deploring such havoc, it must almost be judged to have been a military necessity.

If New York, where the Copperheads were all-powerful, if Washington and Philadelphia had not been ruled with an iron hand, civil war would have broken out in the North. In 1864, when the re-election of Mr. Lincoln hung in the balance, energetic precautions had to be taken. Discretionary powers were given to Butler, known for his rigor. Thirty-thousand men were concentrated in the city. Monitors, with their artillery, were lined up in the harbor, and the elections passed off quietly; even so, the results were abominable: thirty-nine thousand votes were registered against Lincoln.

Difficulties are not yet over. Act second is only just

beginning. No one can yet calculate the extent of the social revolution in the South. I am trying to look into that question. I believe sincerely that only one sort of government could succeed there now: that is to say a military one. So, as you see, I am far from agreeing with M. de Montalembert's article. Such is my fixed opinion. Any other kind of government would lead to mob rule because it would be too weak to prevent popular violence. Nothing is further from my temperament than to advise military domination rather than civil government; but considering the present state of upheaval in the South—no more nor less than a state of war—it cannot be governed civilly. Reflecting on what I have been witness to in this country, I am positive that I am right. It would take at least two volumes for me to develop and comment on recent experiences. As you know, I have always been radical at heart; my ideas have not been modified; on the contrary, they are strengthened. I believe more firmly than ever in a democratic form of government. However, I am less certain than I used to be that one man can exercise control in a community. I am convinced to a greater degree, as days pass, that a Republican form of government is by far the best, but it is not applicable to all peoples and notably, in my opinion, is not consistent with French character. The essential qualities which make a republic great are wanting in our country.[1]

June 30th

We have arrived at the peak temperature of which Washington is capable, that is from forty-eight to fifty degrees centigrade, twice what is ever registered in Paris. Under these conditions, it is necessary to get up with the sun and work until midday; after that, until four in the afternoon, no work is possible; so between four and nightfall work might begin again, but the trouble is that after eight gaslight in a room is unbearable. All the insects come in and it is like being in a zoo. Besides, gas heats so much that if the windows are kept shut it is more insupportable than in the daytime.

Washington is reputed to be the hottest place in America; to find anything worse you would have to go

---

[1] My father, opposed as he was to the Imperialist Government in France and a fervent advocate of democracy elsewhere, was particularly interested in studying the practical working of the executive power in the United States with its immense prerogatives. He believed that these did not constitute the slightest danger to the Republic because they were so admirably counterbalanced by the rights of the States which form the Union. In France, a single nation, no such moderating influence exists, and he came to the conclusion that the best and safest regime there and one which would come nearer the American conception than any other, was a constitutional monarchy resembling that of England.

to the tropics. Up to now I have stood the climate pretty well and suffer less than most people, but I confess that if it continues much longer I shall seek a few days' relief in Boston. I choose Boston because Sumner is there and we can continue discoursing about politics, which will help me to go on with my work.

However, before leaving I want to finish my report on the South. The Boston point of view would do nothing to help me in forming my opinions on this subject, Massachusetts being the very hotbed of abolitionism.

I have been inquiring about the most favorable time for a person who is unaccustomed to this climate to come over and am told by all the doctors consulted that September is the very earliest moment possible. From September on the temperature moderates. I let you know this at once so that you will not be tempted to make plans which might be imprudent. Unnecessary to insist on prudence. I need not say any more except to tell you what a joy it was to see a scrap of your handwriting added to your mother's happy announcement. . . .

HERE ENDS the correspondence of my father to my mother. His American activities, however, were not to cease—far from it. What he had to tell her thenceforth could be communicated orally. My father had reached the decision to bring his wife and children to America. While in Paris, he arranged his official status. He was appointed legal counsellor to the French Legation and also asked to take up the defense of his compatriots' interests in the International Claims Commission, instituted by Senator Sumner during the War. Thus happily reunited in a land dear to both, my parents made for us children a modest but most happy American home.

A. DE C.